Tips for Traveling Salesmen

By
HERBERT N. CASSON

B. C. FORBES PUBLISHING CO.
120 Fifth Avenue - - - New York

COPYRIGHT, 1927, BY
B. C. FORBES PUBLISHING COMPANY

PRINTED IN THE UNITED STATES OF AMERICA

PREFACE

THIS book is, I believe, the first one of its kind for traveling salesmen. Scores of books have been written, in a general way, about salesmanship; but none has been written directly for the salesman on the road.

The work of a traveling salesman is entirely different from the work of any one else. The goodwill of a concern, as well as the profits, depends mainly upon the skill of the traveling salesman.

In fact, the function of the traveling salesman has never yet been fully appreciated. He is usually treated as a mere carrier of samples, whereas he is no such thing. He is the business-getter and goodwill builder of his house or corporation. He is a creator of new business and a conserver of what has already been done.

To know his goods is only the A.B.C. of a traveling salesman's technique. He must know human nature, too, and how to deal with all sorts and conditions of men.

No one, I venture to say, can be too wise or too competent for the position of traveling salesman; and most of us who have been on the road have fallen far short of our possibilities.

This book is offered, therefore, to all sales managers and traveling salesmen in the hope that it may enable them to sell more goods more easily and pleasantly.

THE AUTHOR

CONTENTS

CHAPTER I
BEGIN BY TALKING HIM   3
    Learn Your Customers' Hobbies, Personal Likes and Dislikes — Base Your Approach on These — Then Show Goods.

CHAPTER II
USE MORE EAR AND LESS TONGUE   15
    Give Your Customer the Center of the Stage — The Main Thing Is Not to Talk, but to Sell.

CHAPTER III
PUT SERVICE BEFORE SAMPLES   27
    Study Your Customer's Problems and Needs — Try to Help Him to Move His Goods.

CHAPTER IV
MENTION QUALITY BEFORE PRICE   41
    You Must Know Your Goods Through and Through — Art of Dramatizing a Sale.

CHAPTER V
DON'T TAKE "NO" FOR A FINAL ANSWER .   53
    Difference Between Making and Taking a Sale — Some Examples of Real Salesmanship.

Contents

CHAPTER VI
GET DOWN TO BRASS TACKS QUICKLY . . 65
Watch for Chance to Talk Details of Delivery — Technique of Making a Sale.

CHAPTER VII
BUILD GOODWILL FOR YOUR FIRM 75
Sell Your Company as Well as Your Goods — How to Earn Promotion.

CHAPTER VIII
CONSTANTLY SEARCH FOR NEW MARKETS . 87
Make Several Missionary Calls Every Week — Don't Become a Jog-Trotter.

CHAPTER IX
CLASSIFY YOUR TIME 99
How to Value the Different Hours of the Day — The Best Time to Make a Sale.

CHAPTER X
KEEP MENTALLY AND PHYSICALLY FIT . . 111
Vaccinate Yourself Against Worries — Your Job Is Not a Routine One — It Is All Creative Work.

CHAPTER XI
HAVE A STOUT HEART 123
Be a Bit of a Philosopher — Buck Up Your Customers — A Tip to Wives and Sales Managers.

CHAPTER XII
CREATE WELCOMES FOR YOURSELF 135
Turn Your Customers Into Friends — Keep Your Selling On a Personal Basis.

I

BEGIN BY TALKING HIM

Chapter I

BEGIN BY TALKING HIM

Learn Your Customers' Hobbies, Personal Likes and Dislikes — Base Your Approach on These — Then Show Goods

THE first commandment of traveling salesmen is: "Thou shalt not enter as an unwelcome intruder."

A salesman is not at all like a shop assistant — no such luck. A shop assistant stays in the shop and waits on customers who want to buy; whereas a salesman goes about and tries to sell goods to people who never sent for him.

The salesman enters uninvited. He tries to see a busy man with whom he has no appointment. He is always butting in — forcing himself and his goods upon the attention of people who are thinking of something else.

In the whole world of trade and commerce probably no one has so hard and baffling a job as a traveling salesman. He has to deal with other people, over whom he has no authority. He has to depend absolutely upon his own skill, likeableness, quickness and information. He has a little routine work — mere order-taking. But if he depends on this, he will soon find himself out of a job.

So, as you can see, much depends on how he begins, how he enters a place. The first half-minute may make him or break him.

He can't go in boldly and say: "Well, here I am again. You can't put me out. I have a legal right to come in and I want an order. I must have it, in fact, as I am paid on commission." That entry would be effective, no doubt, on the stage; but it wouldn't do in real life. Neither should a salesman come in timidly and present his card, "I represent Jones and Brown," etc.

All young salesmen start off in that way and find, after a while, that a card carries you nowhere.

No. There is one best way to enter a place and it is remarkable how many travelers are not aware of it.

Every call must be PERSONAL — that is the first rule in salesmanship.

You must prepare before you go in. You must decide beforehand what you are going to do and say. You must be active, not passive; and you must treat every man differently, according to his nature.

Once a big firm trained its travelers to memorize a selling talk. They all said the same thing to everybody. This experiment proved to be a complete failure. It changed the salesmen into poll-parrots. Of course, they failed.

No two dealers are alike, and in the beginning of the sale (not the closing) you must treat each man in a personal way.

You must ask yourself, What is he thinking about? What are his fears — his hopes — his troubles? You must fit into his present line of thought.

One good way to begin your sales talk is to remind him of something he said to you on your last visit. If you have a good memory, you can recall something he said or did. If not, you can make a habit of putting down sayings or events in your notebook.

It is a good plan for every salesman to keep a Card List of his customers, and to put down on these cards any sayings and actions that are worth remembering. Some travelers go as far as to put down on these cards all the fads, beliefs, sports, and so forth of their customers.

On one card, for instance, he may write: " Fond of fishing. Owns a Scotch collie. Goes to the horse races."

On another card he may write: " Keeps a Jersey cow and White Leghorn hens. Has won prizes for hens."

In a word, it is wise to approach a man on the side of his hobbies, rather than his business. He is always more human and accessible on the hobby side.

Then, as soon as you begin to talk business, put something interesting into his hand — something new and special out of your samples.

Sell to his eyes rather than to his ears. Few men are good listeners. While you are talking, their minds are thinking of something else. How can you prevent this? How can you get a man's concentrated attention? By putting something interesting in his hands.

The optic nerve is twenty-two times stronger than the nerve that leads from the ear to the brain. Hence, it follows that what a man SEES has a stronger influence upon him than what he HEARS.

If you will call up in your mind a play that you saw several years ago you will find that you remember the most striking scenes, but not the words.

That is why we must always appeal more to the eye than the ear. And when a customer is holding one of your samples and you are pointing out its qualities you are appealing to *both* eye and ear, and the sense of touch as well. Once you have got as far as this, the worst is over. You will probably get an order. You have won his favorable attention, and unless he is suddenly called away or interrupted he will be likely to buy your goods.

The next point to aim at is the size of the

order. He wants the goods, but the query is: How much?

The customer's mind is now shifting from the goods to the probability of selling them — can he sell a dozen or can he sell four dozen? He is now thinking on right lines and a wise salesman will be quick to think *with* him, instead of showing him other goods, or pointing out the qualities of the goods.

The question now is: What is the possible market for these goods?

If the salesman can say that Blank and Company in Boston sold three dozen in a week, that will be a help.

If he can say that his firm is spending $100,000 advertising these goods in national newspapers and magazines, that, too, will be a help.

If he can say that seventeen firms have re-ordered the goods during the past week, or mention any other fact that will prove the salability of the goods, he will increase the size of his order.

Too many small orders are taken. Of that

Begin by Talking Him

there is no doubt. And the reason is that the salesman did not convince the dealer that the goods were quick sellers.

If the salesman can go further than this and suggest window displays, or advertisements, or any special demonstration, this, also, will help to make his order larger.

The point to remember is that as soon as the customer is interested in the goods, you must talk from His point of view. Talk as a partner. Don't talk about BUYING. Talk about SELLING to the public.

This wipes out all antagonism between you and the customer. It enables you both to aim at one result — the sale of a larger quantity of goods.

You are talking HIM, not your goods — not your firm — not yourself.

A certain salesman of insurance, who sells $2,000,000 of insurance a year, follows out this plan to a remarkable degree.

Before he approaches a man, he learns as much as possible about the man's business, health, family, ambitions, temperament, etc

Then he prepares a plan of insurance that will best suit this man. He works out the man's point of view. Then, not before, he goes to him and says: " How would you like to have a plan of insurance like this? "

If a man has two sons at school, for instance, this salesman says to him: " How would you like to be sure, in case you die next week, that your two sons would have enough money to complete their education, and $5,000 apiece when they are 21? "

As you see, he talks HIM. He compels attention. He almost compels the sale of a policy. He is almost irresistible, because he comes to the prospect from the prospect's point of view.

He treats his customer as a CLIENT, not merely as a Buyer. He does it sincerely. He does not try to over-sell.

If you go into a small shop, begin by BUYING something. Why not? It will be a dollar well spent. If you go into a large shop, begin by appreciating the goods now on sale, or the **window** display.

Begin by Talking Him

Don't come charging down on a man as a salesman.

Don't make him put his hands up and prepare for a fight.

Don't thrust YOUR point of view on him. Don't attack. Don't coerce. Don't launch a selling talk at him as if you were trying to torpedo him into giving you an order.

Your customer is not an enemy. His interests are, in the long run, the same as yours. He is your partner, your friend. You are a fellow-salesman and you are both interested in selling more and more goods to the public.

BEGIN BY TALKING HIM.

II
USE MORE EAR AND LESS TONGUE

Chapter II

USE MORE EAR AND LESS TONGUE

Give Your Customer the Center of the Stage — The Main Thing Is Not to Talk, but to Sell

A TRAVELING salesman is not a lecturer and a customer is not an audience. There is a fact that will greatly increase the selling efficiency of any salesman who is clever enough to see the force of it.

Too much talk! That's what kills customers. Many a manufacturer might have a cemetery at the back of his factory. And on most of the gravestones you would see this epitaph:

" Sacred to the memory of J. B. Jones, Inc., — formerly a customer, but talked to death by one of our travelers."

Most travelers fancy that they are paid to talk. They are not. They are paid to SELL — quite a different thing.

They drown their customers in a flood of talk; and then go to bed without a guilty conscience.

Talk! Argue! Prove! That is their idea of salesmanship, and it is quite wrong. I am pointing out a better way: Listen! Agree! Serve!

In a shop, once, I heard a traveling salesman say to the storekeeper: " You can't deny that, can you? "

Such a man, you see, was entirely misplaced as a salesman. He should have been a Policeman or a Night-watchman.

Isn't it true that most salesmen have the wrong idea of a customer? Their ideal customer is one who listens mutely, and at every pause says, " Send me three dozen." A sort of tongue-tied, easily persuaded man with an inexhaustible bank account — he is their ideal of a perfect customer.

Maybe he would be, but — there are very few such men. Most customers would sooner talk than listen and they abhor writing checks above all things.

The fact is that a salesman ought to encourage the customer to talk. The more the customer talks, at first, the better. A man is like a barrel — you must empty him before you can fill him.

A wise salesman will draw his customer out. He will ask questions — all manner of questions.

If he happens in the shop before the holidays, he will ask the customer where he is going this Summer. And if he happens in after the holidays, he will ask the customer if he has had a pleasant vacation.

He will, in a word, give the customer the center of the stage. He — the salesman — will become the audience.

This is not what the customer expects. It is a welcome change. It gives the salesman a running start.

A salesman should ask his customer questions for two reasons:

1. In order to win the favorable attention and goodwill of the customer.

2. In order to learn the opinions of the cus-

tomer about the goods and the preferences of the public.

One of a salesman's duties is to keep his concern in touch with the customers and the public. If he does this well, he can almost double his value to his employer. He can, eventually, become the sales manager if he learns how to suit the public.

A salesman must be a learner, as well as a teacher. He must avoid that air of superiority that some salesmen possess. He must not be a Know-it-all. And he must suppress the natural tendency that most men have to show off.

A really skilled and ripened salesman will draw out the knowledge of his customer. He will play second fiddle in the conversation, with an eye single to a big order. Very few salesmen — perhaps not one in a hundred — can reach this point of skill and self-control; but it is well worth reaching.

From the point of view of psychology, too, there is a good reason for encouraging the customer to talk.

Most merchants are in a state of suppressed

Use More Ear and Less Tongue

irritation or discouragement. They cannot often talk freely to their own customers. They bottle up their discontent. This makes them abnormal — perhaps morbid or irascible.

It certainly prevents them from buying goods.

Consequently, one of the first steps in the process of selling is to let the customer give free vent to his suppressed fears and complaints.

Talking about his own difficulties normalizes him. That is what we learn from Freud, of Vienna.

Get the poison out — that is how to restore a man to normalcy. Let him talk. Let him talk himself into a better humor and a better attitude towards the world. Then, when he cracks a joke and lights his cigar, the time has come to sell him goods.

As you can see, this is revolutionary. It is not taught by the professors of salesmanship, nor in the courses of study. It is new. It is precisely the opposite of what most traveling salesmen do, especially the younger ones.

The sales talk, that we hear so much about, is not indispensable.

The thrusting, forceful, dominating, spellbinding salesman is a crude specimen, and only fitted to sell to crude people.

A first-class salesman need not even be a good conversationalist. He may be a poor talker — not glib at all; and he may send in twice as many orders as the glibbest man in his firm.

Nearly all our books and courses on Salesmanship have been putting the emphasis on the wrong place. The main thing is not to talk, but to SELL.

So, if more goods can be sold by listening than by talking, then we must listen. We must put a check on the ready tongue and we must use the reluctant ear.

Few men are silent and taciturn. Certainly, few merchants are. Nine out of ten enjoy talking about their own affairs with a friendly outsider. A man can say to a visitor many things that he will not like to admit to his fellow-citizens.

A wise, sympathetic salesman, as a listener, is a boon to many a merchant, who is compelled to put on a bold front to his own family, employees and fellow-citizens.

A safe and sensible man, to whom one can talk freely, is often a godsend to a merchant who has suppressed his complaints to the point of explosion.

A salesman should listen to the flow of pent-up troubles, not because it is his professional duty to do so, but because as a salesman he is interested in people and their affairs.

A salesman is not like an engineer, a draughtsman, an inventor, a designer. He must not have a great power of concentration, as these men have.

Few people can listen courteously, instead of impatiently, or formally. Most people ENDURE rather than listen. They listen because they must, not because they take a pleasure in listening.

But you may have noticed that the most popular man in any club is the one who is the best listener. He is the one who will have the largest funeral, you may be sure of that.

On the other hand, the man who is the bore of any club is the man who insists upon doing most of the talking. He is the room-emptier, the chaser.

One definition of a bore is: A man who keeps on talking about himself when you want to talk about yourself — a very correct definition.

This definition would include the average traveling salesman, as his main idea is to monopolize the talking, and to talk about his concern and his goods.

To bore a customer — how does that help to sell goods? Of what use is it to talk to a man who is thinking of something else? And of what use is it to show samples to a man who is regarding you as a nuisance?

None. The actual process of selling should not begin until you have secured the favorable interest of the customer, and this you do by talking HIM and by listening to him.

No jockey makes his horse do its utmost at

the start; and neither will any competent salesman try to sell goods at the start.

On the contrary, he will do his best to efface himself and to bring his customer to the front, at first.

He will remember that wise saying, " Blessed are the meek, for they shall inherit the earth."

He will remember that courtesy always comes first, and that courtesy consists of a sympathetic interest in the affairs of others.

He will meet every customer as man to man, or friend to friend, before they become seller and buyer. It pays — and it's right.

III

PUT SERVICE BEFORE SAMPLES

Chapter III

PUT SERVICE BEFORE SAMPLES

Study Your Customer's Problems and Needs — Try to Help Him to Move His Goods

EVERY traveling salesman carries samples, but how many carry service? Possibly not one out of fifty — not 2 per cent.

The man who carries service is exceptional. He stands high. He stands at the top of his profession. He is the latest and highest type of salesman.

Long ago, when business was greedier than it is to-day, a salesman's motto was: " Study my own pocket."

Then he grew wiser. He found greediness didn't pay, and he learned a new motto — " Study my goods."

Recently a few salesmen — not many — have gone further still. They have formed a still better motto: "STUDY MY CUSTOMER'S PROBLEMS."

This is the highest point of salesmanship, and very few ever reach it.

After you have listened to your customer's talk — after you have had a personal opening, then you settle down to business and show him how to re-sell your goods.

Almost invariably a retailer needs help or advice. Few retailers know as much about their own business as they should.

The retailer does not want any more dead stock. He has a dread of skilled salesmen who over-sell him. The burnt child dreads the fire; and he has often been burnt.

He is a worried, flurried, hurried man. He is not thinking about you and your goods. He is thinking about bad debts and old stock, and bills payable, and his wife's disposition, and his competitors.

So, when you go into a shop, don't march up with a stiff tread, like a sheriff, and plague the poor shopkeeper with your demands for his personal attention.

Go and look at his stock. See what he

Put Service Before Samples

lacks. Study out his stock situation. Then go and talk to him about it, when he is ready to talk business.

Do try to get it into your mind that the shopkeeper has not been lying awake nights, waiting for the glorious arrival of yourself and your wonderful samples. He has not. He does not regard your samples as a rival show to the Follies. He wouldn't pay a penny admission to see all you've got. So, you must shift your point of view from Samples to Service.

As soon as you go into a shop don't idle about and wait to see your customer. Get busy. Act like a new employee. Act like a worthwhile son-in-law. Help to dress one of the windows. Talk to the shop assistants. Find out the shop news. Show them a new method of display. Take a friendly, practical interest in getting the goods sold to the public.

Be active, not passive. Be positive, not negative. Lend a hand. Give a half-hour's actual service. Then bring on your samples.

A traveling salesman, in fact, must have a

larger idea of himself and his job. He is not merely an order-taker. Neither is he merely a salemaker. A better word for him would be a distributor.

He sells to people who sell again — that is the point to remember at the moment.

His aim is not merely to put more goods on a retailer's shelves, if he is a wise, far-sighted salesman, doing his best to make permanent patrons.

His aim is rather to help the retailer to sell the goods to the public. He is not really selling To the retailer, but THROUGH him, to the consumers.

When a retailer buys goods, they are only HALF sold. They must be re-sold to their final owners.

There are two steps in a sale, or three. When a manufacturer sells to a wholesaler, who sells to a retailer, who sells to the public, there are three steps in the sale.

If the goods remain unsold on the shelves of the retailer, the salesman who sold them is less likely to receive another order.

Put Service Before Samples

So, a salesman does not say to a retailer: "I want to sell you some goods." No. He says: "I want you to sell some goods"—a vastly different thing.

As soon as he works from this point of view he becomes the retailer's best friend. The retailer is no longer afraid of him. He has made the retailer a client, not merely a customer.

This new point of view will be accepted only by the ablest and most intelligent salesmen. The others will say: "Am I my brother's keeper?" They will be afraid that this means more work.

They will say: "It is none of my business whether a retailer sells his stock or not."

The average salesman may not see that when he helps the retailer he helps himself as well. The best way to make retailers buy more is to help them to sell more. That is a fact that cannot be denied.

Let us carry the subject up a bit higher. Let us think about TURNOVER. Few travelers do.

Turnover means how quickly a retailer sells his goods. A jeweler, for instance, turns over his goods once a year, while a grocer turns over his goods about twelve times a year.

Butchers and greengrocers and florists and dairies have a quick turnover. A newsboy has the quickest turnover of all, as he sells out his stock twice a day — morning and evening.

The quicker the turnover, the less capital you need to do a certain amount of business.

A retailer can practically double his capital, without borrowing or investing, if he doubles his turnover.

Goods that sell slowly are the bane of all retailers. They tie capital up. They pull down profits. They often wipe out profits altogether.

There you have the reasons for Special Sales — goods that stick. When a wise retailer finds that he cannot sell a certain line of goods at a profit, he sells them at cost so as to get his money back. But that sort of an adventure makes no profit for anyone.

There are too many cut-price sales — all retailers know that. Far too much merchandise is sold at a loss. It was either wrongly bought or badly sold. The blame lay somewhere between the salesmen and the retailer; and an efficient traveler, instead of trying to dodge the blame, will freely shoulder his share of it. He will do all he can to help the retailer to re-sell.

A traveler, you see, is a professional salesman. He is a specialist on sales. He does nothing else but sell.

A retailer, on the contrary, has to do all sorts of things. He has to be a financier, an employer, an owner of buildings and motorcars and merchandise.

A retailer usually has so many miscellaneous worries that he does not pay enough attention to salesmanship and window display. He has so much routine work that he neglects special sales efforts.

A salesman, consequently, can show him how to dress his windows more effectively. He can tell him what certain New York merchants are doing.

He can show him several ways of pushing dead goods, such as putting them on a table ten feet from the front door, or having the cleverest salesgirl give a demonstration, or making a special offer to sell on instalments.

He may even go further than this and show him how to collect his slow accounts. No one knows how to do this perfectly, but a retailer usually does it very awkwardly.

The problem is how to write a sharp but tactful letter that will bring in the money without offending the customer.

A salesman should have some samples of such letters in his pockets — letters that have been tried by other firms with good results.

I once met one wise salesman who helps retailers with their Income Tax perplexities. Many retailers are paying more than the law requires, as tax collectors have no conscience in these matters. So, this salesman had studied the law carefully, and he could tell a retailer of all the rebates or exemptions that are legal.

As you may imagine, a salesman who can save a retailer $200 taxes a year will not depend upon his samples for his orders.

In such ways as these, and many others, a

Put Service Before Samples

traveling salesman may become a wise counselor to his retailers.

He sincerely concerns himself with any matter that promotes the welfare of his customers — that is the point.

" But," a Sales Manager may say, " all this takes time. How can a traveler cover his territory if he treats customers as clients and partners? "

The answer is: The size of the orders is more important than the number of visits. A traveling salesman is too often regarded as a mere postman — a mere legger — dashing quickly from door to door and collecting the greatest possible number of refusals.

It is better to make one sale in 40 minutes than it is to be given four refusals in an hour. Four times nothing is nothing.

When I was a lad in a retail shop, in the early '80s, in a remote village in Canada, the coming of a traveling salesman was a great event. He remained in the village a day and that day was one of the few shining days of the year.

Always, he entertained us. He told us the

stories and gossip of the big world, which we had never seen.

He was full of fun, wisdom, news, ideas, personal talk. In the evening, we all gathered in the little hotel and listened to him until 10 o'clock, when all good villagers went to bed.

That man was my ideal traveling salesman and is still. Why should his type be abolished? Why should we now have bloodless clerks as travelers, thrusting their unwelcome cards and samples into the faces of retailers and dashing for the next train?

Why can we not restore the profession of traveling salesman to its former height of sociability and service? Any firm that dares to do this will double its sales in two years.

Once, when I was 14, a traveler showed me the one right way to wrap a parcel — pressing the paper towards the edges — making tight corners instead of baggy ones.

Another traveler showed me the conjurer's art of putting a coin on my hand, head up, and turning it upside down on the counter, still with the head up. What boy would ever forget such things?

All this was putting Service before Samples. It was selling goods in a friendly, helpful, human way. It was EFFICIENT SALESMANSHIP, of a kind that is now rare in these days of big organizations.

We should lose no time in getting back to it.

IV

MENTION QUALITY BEFORE PRICE

Chapter IV

MENTION QUALITY BEFORE PRICE

You Must Know Your Goods Through and Through — Art of Dramatizing a Sale

THOUSANDS of sales are lost every year — perhaps hundreds of thousands — because the salesman mentions price first.

These price tellers! They are in almost every retail shop. They are everywhere. You will even find them — dozens of them — in the ranks of traveling salesmen.

You will find it a rule that if a salesman at once tells you the price of an article, it is a sign he knows nothing about the article itself.

And what could possibly be more foolish than to hurl the price at a customer before he has time to see the value of the goods?

Why tell him what he must PAY, before you show him what he will GET?

Why make haste to tell him what he will LOSE, before he knows what he will GAIN?

The real professional rule, as every skilled salesman knows, is: Never mention price until the customer thinks it is more.

If the customer at once asks the price, do not tell him. Say: "Wait a moment. I want to surprise you. Look at the goods first, so that you will see what you're getting for the money." Then, when you have given him a high opinion of the goods, tell him the price.

The customer, naturally, thinks mainly of price. You must not accept his point of view. You must think mainly of the value of the goods.

If you are selling watches, for instance, you will first hand a watch to the customer. Then you will point out its good qualities until the customer thinks it is $10. Then you tell him the price is $7. And you are sure to make a sale.

But if, on the contrary, he glances at the watch and thinks it is worth $5, and if you tell him at once that the price is $7, he will not

Mention Quality Before Price

give you an order. "It is too dear," he thinks. He sees himself losing $2 per watch.

In every sale a great deal of the technique consists in doing first things first; and telling the price comes at the end of the selling process, never at the beginning.

If you must mention a figure at the beginning of the conversation, mention a higher figure. Say: " Now, here is a regular $2 line, as you can see. Notice the workmanship. Hold it up to the light. And I can let you have it for $1.50. It ought to sell easily at $2.75."

You are talking to him in terms of quality and profit. You are showing him what he will make, not what he will have to pay you. That is the correct way.

Price, you see, is mental. It is dear if the customer thinks it is; and it is cheap if the customer thinks it is.

A customer who will object to paying an extra nickel for a bottle of ink will gladly pay $25 for a seat at a prize-fight.

A wealthy woman who will object to paying what she thinks is a 10-cent overcharge on a laundry bill will joyfully pay $150 for an antique chair.

A man will go and buy an automobile for the price of a 7-room house, and he will not for a moment think that the car is dear. He is so keen to have it that he writes out the check cheerfully.

It is a curious fact that people will pay a high price for luxuries, while they hold tight to every cent when they are buying necessities.

They make far more fuss about the price of a cabbage than they do about the price of a bottle of wine. They will pay $5 for a theater ticket much more readily than they will pay 60 cents for a pound of sausages.

It is not the amount of the price that matters. It is the way the customer feels about it.

Consequently, before mentioning price, you must get him into a mood of desire. You must prepare his mind before you give him the price. All this seems simple enough, but it is not done in 90 per cent. of the selling, either by travelers or store clerks.

The reason that it is not done, is because

the salesman does not know much about his goods, and, to tell the truth, is somewhat bored and fed up with them.

The traveler must know his goods through and through — how they are made, the wonderful machines that made them, how they compare with competitive goods, how they wear and the distinguished people who are now using them.

He must have a certain amount of enthusiasm for his goods — the more the better.

A true salesman, in fact, compels the customer to appreciate the goods. He gives the point of view of the goods. He points out the pleasures of ownership. He is the Spokesman of the goods.

When he is selling a fur coat, for instance, he says what the coat would say for itself if it had a voice. He points out that a fur coat is the queen of women's garments. He shows that it is more than fur — more than a coat. It gives a higher social status to the fortunate woman who wears it.

That is why a salesman must have a trained

imagination. He must see what the customer does not see, and he must be able to make the customer see what he sees. He must be able to wake up the customer out of his daze, and compel him to appreciate the merits and the marvels of the goods.

A salesman must not only TALK about quality. He must dramatize it. He must prove it. He must show by test and demonstration the superior quality of his goods.

Very often, the goods are better than they look. A first glance at them does not tell you how valuable they are.

Once, for instance, I was called in to plan a campaign to sell etchings by a famous French artist. These etchings were very valuable, but the artist's name was unknown in Britain and America.

At first glance, these etchings looked outrageously dear and the salesmen reported that the price was far too high.

So, to demonstrate their value, I had a special picture frame made for every salesman. At the top of each frame were three high-

Mention Quality Before Price 47

power electric lights under a hood. And the etchings could be readily put in these frames, or taken out.

The salesmen were offering the etchings direct to business men, for their homes. They were not trying to sell to dealers.

Armed with a hooded frame, a salesman would go into a business man's office, pull down the curtains, connect the frame with an electric light, and, in a darkened room, a blaze of light would fall directly upon the etching.

This is what we call dramatizing a sale. It creates curiosity, appreciation, desire. It is not a trick. It is a legitimate device to display goods of high quality. In this case, we sold all our etchings, at a slightly higher price.

A customer, may I say, is one who wants the goods more often than he wants the price. There is the central fact around which all Salesmanship is built.

How to increase the " want " of the customer, in some other way than by lowering the price — that is the problem.

To make a sale by cutting the price — to

make a sale by giving away the profit — is not salesmanship at all. If persevered in, it is bankruptcy.

Salesmanship means selling goods at a fair profit to customers who are satisfied.

There is a pair of scales, as we might say, in the customer's mind. On the one side of the scales there is the price and on the other side is the article to be sold.

What, then, can be done to tip the scales in favor of the article? That is the vital point.

Every well-made article has a definite number of quality-points of design, style, durability, limited quantity, new features, etc. The salesman must have these at the tip of his tongue.

Quality, in a word, is like a ladder. It has different rungs, or grades, like this:

- Artistic.
- Original.
- Superior.
- Good.
- Good Enough.
- Half Good.
- No Good.

The great bulk of cheap goods are " good enough." They have a few quality-points, not many.

But " good " merchandise has points of quality that must be pointed out, if it is to be sold.

The tragedy of merchandising is to be compelled to sell " good " merchandise at " good enough " prices. That happens for lack of salesmanship.

The price goes up by leaps and bounds when you move towards the top of the ladder. An " artistic " gown is worth ten times the price of a " good " gown, for instance. The Paris dressmakers know that.

Just as a chess player works out new moves to beat his opponent — just as a jockey works out a better way to handle a difficult horse — so a salesman must work out new ways of showing the quality of his goods, so that, when he tells the price, the customer will prefer the goods to the money.

V

DON'T TAKE "NO" FOR A FINAL ANSWER

Chapter V

DON'T TAKE "NO" FOR A FINAL ANSWER

Difference Between Making and Taking a Sale — Some Examples of Real Salesmanship

"CAN I sell you anything to-day?" said a traveling salesman to a shopkeeper.

"No," replied the shopkeeper.

"All right," replied the traveler, "I'll call next month. Good morning!" And out he went.

That sort of thing is supposed to be called SALESMANSHIP.

That traveler may even have had a belief that it was his DUTY to leave as soon as the shopkeeper said "No."

He took "No" as his cue to go out, whereas, if he had been a trained salesman, he would have taken "No" as his cue to BEGIN SELLING.

The fact is, that real professional salesmanship starts when the customer says " No."

If a customer says " Yes," then no salesmanship is needed. Any order-taker will do.

THE WHOLE OBJECT OF SALESMANSHIP IS TO CHANGE NEGATIVES INTO AFFIRMATIVES.

If a salesman cannot face a " No " and change it into a " Yes," then he is a round peg in a square hole.

Salesmanship is persuasion. It is the overcoming of difficulties. It is an advance in the face of an attack.

There is an element of WAR in salesmanship, but with this great difference — the customer must not be forced to do what he will regret.

A professional salesman conquers a customer by taking the customer's point of view. He shows the shopkeeper how to sell. He cheers up the shopkeeper and gives him a plan for selling more goods.

A real salesman is the shopkeeper's best friend. He comes to the shopkeeper as a man comes to a run-down clock. He cleans the discouragement out of his mind, winds him up and starts him going.

THE MAN WE NEED AT THE MOMENT, MORE THAN ANYONE ELSE, IS THE SALESMAN WHO CAN CHANGE "NO" INTO "YES" AND START THE WHEELS OF TRADE SPINNING AT FULL SPEED.

"The best sale I ever made," said W. S. English, a well-known traveler, "was on one occasion when I turned a man's 'No' into 'Yes.'

"I was selling gas mantles. My firm made a good mantle, but did not advertise very much. Their mantles had more quality than fame.

"My firm was very anxious to sell to a certain Mr. Long. He had steadfastly refused to buy from us, as he was a regular customer of a rival firm.

"I went to Mr. Long, gave him the usual sales talk. No result. He said: 'I'll make up my mind this evening. Call on me to-morrow morning at 9 o'clock and I will give you my decision.'

"Of course, I knew what that meant. It meant 'No.' He was trying to let me down easy.

"I made up my mind that I must do something different. I felt sure that Mr. Long was not convinced of the quality of our mantles.

"I had only TALKED about quality, but I hadn't proved it. This seemed to me to be the weakness of my salesmanship.

"I pondered over the matter for two hours. Then I had an idea. It flashed on my mind like a gleam of light.

"I rushed out of the hotel and bought a pair of apothecary scales, and an assortment of mantles of various makes.

"Then, next morning at 9 o'clock, I went to see Mr. Long. As I had expected, he said 'No.'

"I didn't fade away as most salesmen do when they get struck by a 'No.' I said: 'Very well, Mr. Long, but if I can prove to you that price for price my mantles are the best, will you reconsider your decision?'

"He was kind enough to agree, so we went into his office. I took out my scales and all the mantles.

"One by one I weighed the mantles. Then I burned them and re-weighed them.

"I was taking a chance on what the result would be, but I had faith in my firm. I knew that our factory put quality first.

"When we compared figures, I had proved my case. Our mantles had more actual thorium and cerium oxide than those of our competitors. Price for price, ours were plainly the best.

"Mr. Long was convinced. He said 'Yes,' and I went off at 10 o'clock with an order for 10,000 mantles."

There is a vast difference, as you can see, between MAKING a sale and merely TAKING it.

When a customer wants to buy before you come to him, that is only TAKING a sale; but when he didn't think of buying until you showed him that he ought to, that is MAKING a sale.

On one occasion a young salesman, who sells

furniture for a wholesale house, went into a mining town.

He found that the largest shop in town was packed full of goods, and, also, he found that the shopkeeper was packed full of the blues.

"Well," said the salesman, "I see I can't sell you anything, but perhaps I can help you to get rid of all this stuff.

"Let's take half-a-dozen phonographs in a motor truck and sell them to the miners."

They motored to a mining village fifteen miles away and sold five phonographs. The next day they sold twelve in other villages.

The salesman went away with a $1,500 order. That was a case of MAKING a sale.

Here is another case. A biscuit salesman had tried for two years to sell his goods to the chief grocer in a New England town, but without success.

At last, the light broke in on his mind. He saw that he must MAKE a sale, not take it.

He went into this grocer's shop and asked — "Will you sell a carload of biscuits for us, Mr. Gray?"

Mr. Gray was swept off his feet. Of course, he would sell a carload of biscuits, but how?

The salesman had a Plan — a one week BISCUIT SALE, prepared for by a week of free samples.

The grocer wrote an order for half a carload, sold it all and ordered more. That sale was MADE, not taken.

The fact is, that nine salesmen out of ten approach a dealer in the wrong way. They talk BUYING not SELLING. There is a world of difference, if you'll give it a moment of thought. When a dealer BUYS, he pays out money. But when he SELLS, he takes in money.

That is why no dealer likes to talk about buying, and why every dealer loves to talk about selling.

If you want to learn the profitable art of MAKING sales, you must study your customer's point of view.

Making a sale doesn't mean compelling a customer to take what he doesn't want. It means getting him to appreciate the goods and to see what he can do with them.

A salesman who was selling plots of land was given 48 plots to sell near a beach. The land was eight minutes' walk from the station.

The salesman walked his prospects to the plots and then took them down to the beach, a quarter of a mile distant.

Nobody bought. Most of them did not go to the beach. So the salesman changed his methods.

He took each prospect in a taxi to the beach first. He sold them on the beach. Then he showed the plots and walked back to the station.

In a short time he sold all the 48 plots. Those 48 sales were made, not taken.

So, the fact that I wish to make clear is that the SALESMAN MUST BE ACTIVE, CREATIVE, SUGGESTIVE, POSITIVE.

Standing still, looking bored and answering questions as briefly as possible, isn't Salesmanship — not on your life it isn't.

Turning yourself into an imitation of a penny-in-the-slot machine, isn't Salesmanship.

Standing behind a glove counter and wishing

Don't Take "No" for an Answer 61

you could go far away and never see a pair of gloves again as long as you lived, isn't Salesmanship.

Traveling from door to door with a detested bag of samples and fading out as soon as a dealers says "No," isn't Salesmanship.

No, but thousands of sales people think it is. They expect to be paid for this sort of thing.

They would be very much offended if they were paid in Tin money at the end of the week; but they give this sort of Tin Salesmanship to their firms.

They can only TAKE a sale when a customer gives it to them. They cannot MAKE a sale.

They are negative, passive, mechanical and indifferent.

Give us sales people who can make sales and half of our business troubles will disappear.

To sum up, there is always more or less BUYER-RESISTANCE. In good times there is less of it and in bad times there is more. But there is always resistance, and much of it can be overcome.

Thousands of customers say "No" as a

habit. Every experienced salesman knows that. It is a habit of self-protection, or pocket-protection. They say "No" to give themselves time to think.

Therefore, when a man says "No," his refusal should not be taken as final. The conversation may be switched to another subject, but the attempt at selling should not be abandoned.

A salesman should have the perseverance of a scientist. He should be deaf to that disastrous word "No."

He should be like those boxers who fight all the better after they have been knocked down.

He should never forget that a strong man makes a ladder out of his failures, not a wall. He climbs up over obstacles. He does not turn back. He keeps on until the resistance is overcome, or until he finds out that there are good reasons for the resistance.

VI

GET DOWN TO BRASS TACKS QUICKLY

Chapter VI

GET DOWN TO BRASS TACKS QUICKLY

Watch for Chance to Talk — Details of Delivery — Technique of Making a Sale.

TOO many traveling salesmen are like the parrot that " talked too ―― much." They keep on talking when the chance has come to be writing down orders.

Many a salesman talks a customer into a sale and then goes on and talks him out of it.

The right technique in making a sale is this: First listen to the customer, then talk to him about his affairs, from his point of view, then get him interested in your goods.

As soon as he shows desire for your goods, it is wisest to take it for granted that he has made up his mind to buy.

You should then stop pointing out quality.

You should as quickly as lightning change the conversation to details of delivery.

You should ask about assortment or quantity or time of shipment or any other detail, in order to get the customer's mind definitely made up.

To use a simile from the carpenter's trade, you should clinch the nail the moment it comes through the board.

You should say, " I can let you have 10 gross of these." Certainly you must not say, " How many do you want? "

Too often a salesman forces a customer into a corner and compels him to say " Yes " or " No." This shows a lack of skill. It usually makes the customer say " No."

A salesman should take it for granted that the customer wants the goods, just as soon as this seems to be true.

He then says, at once: " Would you prefer to have them sent by motor, instead of by rail? "

" Do you want them for next Monday's Sale? "

Get Down to Brass Tacks Quickly 67

"Shall I send our new Window Display with it?" or any similar question.

A salesman must, in this way, do all that he can to prevent a customer from feeling that he has surrendered.

He must talk as though this were a matter of mutual interest, as indeed it is. He must not assume an attitude of forcing the customer to buy.

One salesman, for instance, who came into my office to sell me a new kind of a typewriter, first secured my interest by a very clever demonstration, and then spoiled it all by saying, "Well, I can't sell you one, can I?" Of course I said "No." If he had said "I can leave this one with you, if you'd like to have it at once," I would probably have bought it.

The fact is that many salesman are good at opening a sale but bad at closing. There are some salesmen so clever that they can get in to see anybody, but after they have got in they do not make a sale. Every big concern has lost money on salesmen of this sort.

They are always men of pleasing appearance, good education and great fluency. They are sociable, too, and quick to make friends.

By means of all these good qualities, they secure an interview. They get favorable attention — and that is all they get.

They have a pleasant conversation which ends in nothing but a " Good-bye! Call again." They go away without an order.

They make hundreds of " almost " sales. They often impress their employers, for a time, as being first-class salesmen. But their order books tell the tale.

They are about 80 per cent. salesmen. If they could only learn to close, to bring matters to a head, they would rise to par.

Favorable attention, you see, is not enough. A salesman must be an entertainer, up to a point. He must appear to be making a social call, if you like, until the psychological moment comes to get the order. Then he must suddenly turn into a man of facts and figures and details.

He must be able to get down to brass tacks in a flash.

Get Down to Brass Tacks Quickly 69

Having a good time with a customer is all very well as far as it goes, but it doesn't go far enough.

If a customer says, " I will let you know next week," or " I'll think it over," that sale is lost, 99 times out of 100. Every experienced salesman knows that.

Promises yield no dividends. They pay no salaries and no profits. Nothing has been done until the order is in the book.

Always, a salesman must do all he can to prevent this postponement of a decision. He must not accept it as the end of the interview.

One very able salesman, for instance, called on a business man and convinced him that he needed a better office equipment. The business man plainly wanted the new equipment, but he was by nature a postponer. He said to the salesman: " This is a large matter. It involves too much money to close at once."

The salesman replied, " Mr. Smith, is it not true that a deal of this size is a mere trifle for your company? Do you really need to postpone it? Can you not decide it right away just as you do other important matters?"

He got the order — he deserved it.

Many a customer has an inbred dislike to saying " Yes." He prefers always to appoint a committee, or to put some of the responsibility on some one else.

He has more authority than experience, probably, as many executives have. This makes him non-committal. He is always aiming at safety rather than net profit.

Many men have vague, hazy brains — twilight brains. Their wills are weak and swayed more by fears than hopes.

As you can see, to sell goods to such brains requires great decisiveness on the part of the salesman. If he, too, is a drifter and a postponer, nothing will be done.

Few customers know their own minds. They act only when pushed. They follow the line of most compulsion and least resistance all through life.

For this reason, a salesman must take con-

Get Down to Brass Tacks Quickly 71

trol of the interview. He must not play second fiddle, although he may seem to be doing so.

A salesman is not a mere conversationalist. He knows when to converse and when to shut up. He uses conversation as a tool.

What he is concerned with is the process that is going on in the mind of the customer. And he is determined that this process shall end in an order.

He is an order-getter, not a propagandist nor a collector of kind words.

In every sale the fewer words the better. Suppose, for instance, that a man is selling his services as an efficiency expert. Suppose that he is called in by a board of directors, whose main idea is to pump him dry and let him go, what should he do?

Certainly, he should not make a sales talk. The odds are against him. They can easily out-talk him. They can make game of him with foolish questions.

He should take it for granted that they want his services. He should say, pleasantly, " Yes,

I shall be glad to do this work for you. I can give you Wednesdays."

He should press them for details as to what, where and when. Then, before any talk can begin, he should pick up his hat and leave.

Almost always, too much time and talk are spent in making a sale. And too many sales are talked off as well as on.

A keen salesman will be on the watch for his chance to ask for the details of delivery.

He will close off the sales interview by a busy five minutes of order-taking. As soon as he has a nibble, he will jerk. That is what I mean.

This one Tip, studied and carried out by any competent salesman, will make two orders grow where only one grew before.

VII

BUILD GOODWILL FOR YOUR FIRM

Chapter VII

BUILD GOODWILL FOR YOUR FIRM

Sell Your Company as Well as Your Goods — How to Earn Promotion

IT goes without saying that a salesman should never let his company down. When he stands in front of a customer, his creed must be: " My company, right or wrong."

If there are any confessions or excuses to be made, let them come from the Sales Manager — from the home office.

A salesman must admit freely what he cannot honestly deny, but he must always defend his firm, just as a lawyer must always defend his client before the judge.

Stand like a rock, if you are met with a flood of complaints.

Don't assume that the customer is right. Assume nothing. Say: " I will have all this investigated; and you may rely upon my company to put matters right."

Never agree with a customer when he blames your house. Many salesmen do, with the intention of pleasing the customer.

Often a salesman will say, in disgust, " There! That is the third time in this week that the clerks in our office have made a blunder — the wooden-heads."

That is what he FEELS like saying. That is probably the truth. But it is not a wise thing to say.

A salesman should try to speak from the point of view of the customer. He should " talk him." But not against his own concern.

The man who lowers his concern lowers himself still more.

For his own sake, a traveling salesman must fight his company's battles and guard its interests.

Even though his customer may feel annoyed at him, at the moment, the customer will respect him all the more for taking the company's part.

A salesman who accepts blame, as though he were the head of the house, is a much larger man to the eyes of the customer than a salesman who joins in the attack on his own company.

Whether you remain with the company or not, no matter. Stand by it as long as its money is in your pocket.

All the world despises a Judas who betrays his Master for 30 pieces of silver; and a man is certainly as bad as Judas when he betrays the concern that has honored him with its confidence and its money.

Loyalty is always and everywhere a virtue that everyone respects. It is a virtue among savage and civilized nations. It has always been a virtue and it always will be. It has not been abolished nor modified by this Age of Trade and Commerce.

"Every man for himself" — yes, up to a point. The question is: Does any man help his own interests by letting his concern down? He does not.

If a salesman finds that his company is dishonest or unreliable, then his one best policy is to resign and find another employer that can be depended upon. No salesman can do good work if he is ashamed of his employer.

A salesman owes it to himself to work for a concern that he can trust and respect.

The best concerns make blunders at times. They send the wrong goods or the wrong bill or something of the sort.

They make clerical errors, or errors that arise from the carelessness of a new employee; and when these mistakes are made, the salesman must stand by his house and insist that all errors will be corrected.

A salesman is never guilty of bad taste when he praises his employer. He is like a football player, who can praise his team without being accused of egotism.

Usually, in sports, it is team-play that makes a team win; and the same fact is true of a business organization.

The spirit of team-play — the company feeling — goes far to make an organization successful.

The salesman who runs away to a competing firm and takes his customers with him, or tries to do so, is not respected, even by the concern that takes him on.

There are rules of fair play and decent conduct in business, just as there are in sport. And, in the long run, the man who breaks these rules suffers for it.

Goodwill! That is the main thing. It is more than money, because it is the basis of credit.

The salesman who builds up his firm's goodwill will soon create a goodwill of his own. That is the vital point to remember.

Every day of his life, a salesman is either increasing or decreasing the goodwill of his company.

By his appearance, his methods, his talk, a salesman is adding to or subtracting from his company's assets. That may not be a comfortable thought. But it is a fact that ought to be remembered.

The traveling salesman who says, proudly, " I have the best employer in the world," does not do himself any damage and he is not set down as a braggart.

To say this is not always easy, especially after he has had a long, fault-finding letter from his Sales Manager, as often happens. But the traveler who can keep his loyalty red-hot, in spite of splashes of cold water, will do well for his employer and himself, both.

Goodwill must come first. It must even come before sales, if there should be any clash between the two.

A sale should never be made at the expense of goodwill — that is a fact that many a concern forgets, when it has dead stock to get rid of.

A traveling salesman, in fact, is much more than a salesman. He really is an agent — an intermediary — a commercial ambassador. There is no word in the English language to properly define him.

He is not merely selling goods. He is building up the reputation of his organization. He is not at all like a door-to-door canvasser, who represents nobody, and whose one aim is to make a sale.

A traveler represents his company. He is the whole company, legally, as he stands in front of a customer. The company is responsible for what he says and does.

The company is the body and he is one of the finger-ends. He is a vital part of his firm. He is not a hireling. He is not a messenger — a carrier of samples.

"I am Brown and Smith, Incorporated," he can truly say.

No other member of the organization is in the same favored position as a traveling salesman. He is not supervised, as a foreman or a shop assistant is.

He is on his own. He does not work in his company's building. He is trusted to regulate his own hours.

He is a free and independent man of business, as long as he does well. He is judged by results.

If he is paid on commission, as he should be, he is practically on the same footing as an owner, although he has not invested any capital in the company. He gets his full fair share of the profits. He is not at all a wage-worker. He takes his own risks, plans and performs his own work and gets all that he earns.

Consequently, as he is practically a partner, he should take a partner's interest in the prosperity of his concern.

He may not always be a salesman. He may become Sales Manager — President. Many a man has climbed up from the position of traveling salesman to the presidency of his firm.

Promotion! That is to be considered, as well as salary and commission. And the way to become a high executive is to act like one and keep it up.

So, it is always a wise policy, after the last order has been taken, to say a few words about your people. Surely there is one sentence that can be said in praise of one's own organization.

" By the way, you may be pleased to know that our new factory is finished," some such news as this will always come to mind.

A man cannot blow his own horn without

being a bit of a bore; but he can blow his company's horn. He can talk for two minutes as though he were its president.

Also, a salesman can serve his company by sending back to the Sales Manager the opinions of customers, or any item of news regarding them.

If a shop is falling into decay, he can mention the fact in one of his letters.

He can take note of any new progressive store and notice whether it is likely to prosper or to be a mushroom growth.

If salesmen did their full duty, there would be fewer of these frauds whereby goods are bought, sold at a low price and never paid for.

A salesman can do much, too, to create public opinion about his organization.

There may be a misunderstanding about it. It may have a bad name, undeservedly, for something it is believed to have done in the past.

During the war, for instance, many concerns were compelled to lower the quality of their goods. They were obliged to use substitutes. Their goodwill was seriously injured. Any such matter as this can be dealt with by traveling salesmen, as they go up and down among the customers.

So, it is clear that a salesman has a wide scope for his efforts, when he tries to sell his organization as well as the goods.

VIII

CONSTANTLY SEARCH FOR NEW MARKETS

Chapter VIII

CONSTANTLY SEARCH FOR NEW MARKETS

Make Several Missionary Calls Every Week — Don't Become a Jog-Trotter

IT is a strange fact that among traveling salesmen the oldest will bring in the fewest new accounts. When a traveler has been nine or ten years with a company he has become well acquainted with its customers. He is made welcome. He is given cigars. The customers listen to his stories; and his business has become largely a matter of visiting his friends.

Consequently, he does not like to dig up new customers. He has become dignified. He is proud of his position as one of the Senior Salesmen of his house. He does not like to have anyone ask him what his name is; and thus he brings in very few new accounts.

A young chap, on the contrary, who has no friends and no dignity and no past career with the company, will usually bring in more new accounts than anybody else.

Once, a firm of jewelers had a contest among its salesmen, to see who could bring in the greatest number of new accounts.

There was a keen young man at the telephone switchboard. He was not a salesman. He had never sold anything in his life.

He asked permission to enter the contest. To please him, the concern agreed. Then, to the amazement of everyone, he won the prize against 30 experienced traveling salesmen.

Naturally, not having any regular customers, this young man went into every jewelery shop. He probably had more refusals than any of the other salesmen, but he opened up the greatest number of new accounts.

You will find it to be a general rule, that the older a salesman is in point of service, the fewer new accounts he will open up.

The old, experienced traveler will generally

Constantly Search for New Markets

bring in the largest orders, but not very many new customers.

He will justify himself by all manner of very clever excuses, but when his place is taken by a younger man, new customers are invariably found. Often, the volume of business is doubled.

He goes into a town and gets $1,000 worth of orders, whereas he might have got $2,000 worth if he had searched for new customers.

Over and over again, concerns have found that plenty of absolutely new business can be dug up in a territory which is supposed to be well canvassed.

Every traveling salesman goes past too many doors. When he arrives in a town, he at once thinks of a certain number of houses. HE MAKES HIS USUAL ROUND — that is the danger that confronts every salesman.

Unless he is on his guard, every traveling salesman becomes more or less an automaton. He gets into a rut. Why? Because a rut is always easier and requires no thought.

Most men prefer the smooth broad path,

that leads nowhere in particular, instead of the rough narrow path that leads upwards to success.

It is a fact, known to everyone, that there are too many jog-trot travelers, jogging from town to town and getting only the easy orders.

They send in just enough orders to keep themselves from being sacked, but nobody makes any profit on them except the railways and hotels.

They take the orders that regular customers give them, and they imagine that they are doing their full duty as salesman.

They never make a fight to get new business. They never invent new ways to makes sales.

Recently I heard a remarkable story about an insurance company that changed its traveling salesmen from jog-trotters to record-breakers. It can be done.

To begin with, this company had 1,700 travelers or salesmen in 1913, who produced $20,000,000 of business.

To-day, it has 375 salesmen, who produced last year $52,000,000.

In 1913, its average salesman produced $11,750 in orders a year.

To-day its average salesman produces $137,325.

The selling power of each salesman was multiplied by eleven.

How was it done?

First, it tested all its traveling salesmen — tested them by studying their records and by personal examination.

It found that its best salesmen were the married ones, 33 to 38 years old, who belonged to a number of organizations and had saved money.

It found that college education was not important, and that the main thing was the ambition and energy and sense of the man himself.

Second, it trained the men that it picked out. It spent, all told, $1,000 on every man to make him highly skilled in the art of salesmanship.

It weeded out the jog-trotters, and to-day its business is 250 per cent. higher than it used to be.

Tests like this prove that every body of

traveling salesmen needs to be kept alive and alert. It must not be allowed to drift along, neither for its own sake nor the company's sake.

There must be a constant search for new markets. If your present distributors are not doing their share, then new distributors must be found.

Stagnation must never be accepted as a normal condition — how few companies realize that!

Every company loses customers. Consequently, every company must secure new customers to make up for their losses. The company that loses fifty customers a year and gains forty is on its way to the graveyard.

There is a word called "saturation," which is doing many concerns a great deal of harm. "We have reached the point of saturation in selling our goods to Detroit," says a Sales Manager.

How does he know? Has he any data or does he merely say this because it pleases the executives?

Constantly Search for New Markets

The point of saturation is not a FIXED point. It depends upon salesmanship. The demand can be doubled — perhaps trebled, by skillful selling and advertising.

You will often hear a salesman say: " No, I never go there. They do not buy from us." He makes this absurd remark as though it were wise — as though it were a legitimate excuse.

Once, when I was traveling, I was having a chat with a traveling salesman. He got off at Chicago.

" Well, good-bye," he said, " I have to see three concerns here."

Why three? The same old three concerns, no doubt, that he had been calling on for five years!

Surely, in a busy city like Chicago there ought to be more than three customers for his goods. Surely he had not saturated Chicago when he made three sales.

On another occasion I asked a manufacturer how many customers he had.

" About 7,000," he replied.

" And how many haven't you got? " I

asked. He was surprised. He didn't know. An investigation was made and it was found that there were 18,000 customers he HADN'T got. Yet he had reached the point of saturation, in his opinion.

So, is it not clear that a traveling salesman must do a certain amount of creative work every week? Is it not clear that he should never let a week go by without an attempt to put new names on his list?

If he is selling to retail shops, he can try several new streets every week. If he is selling to manufacturers, he can follow the line of chimneys, instead of the line of old customers.

It is a wise plan to try experiments on non-customers instead of on regular buyers. There is less to lose if the experiment fails.

In a word, every keen, ambitious traveler must do missionary work for at least half-a-day a week.

He must not allow himself to become like a postman, jogging along from one familiar door to another, as though there were not

Constantly Search for New Markets 95

scores of possible customers whom he is passing by.

For his own sake and his employer's sake, he should develop the possibilities of his territory, and not settle down to the unprofitable opinion that the sales he is making are all that can be made.

Now and then, he might spend a whole week in calling on non-customers and none else. That would be a week well spent.

IX
CLASSIFY YOUR TIME

CHAPTER IX

CLASSIFY YOUR TIME

How to Value the Different Hours of the Day — The Best Time to Make a Sale

A CERTAIN employer called his forty traveling salesmen together recently and made the following speech:

" Gentlemen, I have been making some interesting calculations, which are just as important to you as to me.

" They explain, in fact, why I cannot raise your salaries and why I cannot afford a Roll-Royce this year.

" I find that the actual number of days you worked last year was 265. You average 100 days off for Sundays, holidays and illness.

" Allowing 8 hours a day, this means 2,120 hours. But this is not your actual selling time.

"I find that you have averaged 6 calls a day — 32 calls a week. These calls average 15 minutes each.

"But only half of the calls result in real interviews, so that leaves only 16 interviews a week.

"Only half of these interviews resulted in sales. That means that your actual selling time last year was 8 times 15 minutes or, TWO HOURS A WEEK.

"You are costing me in salaries alone about $50 per hour, apiece, for actual selling time. This seems incredible, but I cannot find any error in these figures. Can any one of you show me where I am wrong?"

The salesmen were silent. There was nothing to be said. It was true.

BUT THE NEXT WEEK THEIR SALES WENT UP 30 PER CENT.

This was an extreme case. But the fact is that the average actual selling time of traveling salesmen is not far from two hours a day.

In a 300-day year, for instance, a traveler usually spends about 75 days in actual selling.

Classify Your Time

He spends 110 days traveling. He is well named a traveler, for he travels more than he sells. He is the railway's best friend. Also, he spends 50 days writing, in offices and lobbies; and 65 days doing clerical work.

"Talk about an 8-hour day," says a Sales Manager. "If I could get my travelers to do a 4-hour day, they would sell twice as much goods as they do now."

And this is not the worst of it.

Not only does a traveler lose 6 hours out of the 8-hour day. Often, he does worse. He loses the BEST 3 hours. He loses the precious time between 12 and 1 and between 2 and 4.

These three hours, in my opinion, are worth almost double as much as the other 5 hours of day.

The PEAK of the day, in value — in possibilities of selling — is the hour between 2 and 3.

THIS IS THE GOLDEN HOUR FOR ALL TRAVELING SALESMEN.

If I were putting a value on the various hours of the day, I would price them as follows:

9 to 10	5
10 to 11	10
11 to 12	20
12 to 1	40
1 to 2	10
2 to 3	60
3 to 4	40
4 to 5	20
5 to 6	10
6 to 7	5

A day ought to be cut up, in fact, in the same way that a butcher cuts up a bullock. Some parts of the bullock will be sold for 40 cents a pound and other parts will be sold for 20 cents a pound.

The hour between 2 and 3 is the one best hour to sell goods for the reason that the customer is feeling more amiable and sociable at that time than at any other hour of the day.

Some men are so irascible that they should never be seen except after lunch. Every experienced salesman knows that. This hour seems to be the only time when some men are human.

After lunch, a business man has got rid of the most pressing worries of the day. He has escaped from his infernal correspondence, with its demands and complaints.

Also, he has had his lunch, and that means that his brain has slowed down. His subconscious brain is giving its attention to his stomach, not to his cerebrum. He is digesting rather than thinking. His mind and his will are relaxed. He is less aggressive and more friendly.

He is easier to approach and to convince. He will listen to you. He will give you his WHOLE mind, not 10 per cent. of it, as he is apt to do if you bother him between 9 and 10.

On the whole, he is rather pleased to see you between 2 and 3, as he is in the humor for a talk with some one.

So the problem, so far as time is concerned, is how to spend the most favorable hours in actual selling.

If a traveler sees no one between 9 and 10, no matter. If he sees no one between 10 and 11 or between 5 and 6, there is little lost. But if he wastes the Golden Hour, from 2 to 3, then more than a quarter of his day has gone.

The secret of an efficient day, to a traveling salesman, is to be actually selling goods from 11 to 1 and from 2 to 4. These 4 precious hours must not be used for traveling, waiting or clerical work.

This new formula, which I am here presenting to traveling salesmen, might be worded as follows:

Classify your time according to its value, and spend the most valuable hours in meeting customers, and not in traveling, waiting and clerical work.

From 2 to 3 is the tidbit of the day. Save it from wastage.

I have heard old buffalo hunters say that they often would kill a buffalo merely for his tongue. They left all the rest of the buffalo to the coyotes. They took only the tidbit, when meat was plentiful.

In the same way, travelers should regard that hour — 2 to 3 — as the most precious bit of the day. They should not waste it, as I have often seen them do, in drowsy siestas in the hotels.

Is it true that the Big Event of the day to many salesmen is the hour from 2 to 3? No. It is the hour and a half from 1 to 2:30. The Big Event is LUNCH.

Lunch is the Peak. It is the comfort — the consolation. Many a salesman anticipates it for 2 hours and regrets it for another 2 hours.

He eats a thick slice of roast beef, two big potatoes, a plate of cabbage and a slice of pie, after which he becomes torpid for an hour. That's what happens to at least the first half of the Golden Hour.

An efficient salesman, on the contrary, eats a light lunch. At 6:30 or 7 P.M., after his day's work is done, he can have his big dinner — as big as he wishes.

A traveler, in a word, must keep himself fit. He is not a routine worker. He is not an automaton. A day's work, to a traveler, is like running a race, or playing a game. It is a contest — brain against brain. That is why he should not gorge himself just before the most important hour of the day arrives.

Whenever possible, he should take a customer to lunch. That will be making a good use of the 1 to 2 hour.

In some trades, the best hour may be 4 to 5, or 10 to 11, but the general principle still holds true. The hours of the day are not alike in value to any salesman.

The use of his time is left to him. He is not like a school teacher, following a schedule, or like a railway engine driver, keeping to a time-table that has been arranged for him.

He should plan his day. Every evening he should plan to-morrow. He should never let a day crash on him unawares.

Many traveling salesmen have grown into the habit of writing off Monday morning and Saturday morning. Nothing can be done, they say, on these two unfortunate mornings.

Neither can they make sales, they believe, before 11 A.M., nor after 5 P.M., nor between 1 and 2; nor when the customer is busy, nor when he is out of temper. These travelers gradually come to an end, because they avoid all the difficulties.

If it is true that certain mornings and hours are of no value as selling hours, then a traveler should manage to do some other work in these hours and concentrate his full selling force into the good hours.

There is no reason why a salesman should waste his traveling time and his waiting time, as many do.

Plans can be made on the train, and in a waiting room. A traveler can always have a book in his pocket — a novel or a text-book.

Many salesmen object to being managed in detail by the home office. Some of them rejoice in their freedom, but they do not make a good use of their freedom.

They are like the young salesman who, when he was first sent out on the road, wrote back home to his mother and said:

"I am my own master and I am taking orders from no one." Very likely.

If a traveler can be set free to manage himself, he will be all the better for it, if he is the right sort. I do not believe in handling travelers as though they were busses — as though they wore pedometers and were paid on mileage. If they are driven to make a fixed number of calls per day, they are apt to be made into nervous wrecks or liars, more likely the latter.

Manage yourself. Then you will not be harried by the home office.

Divide up your day. Use the best hours for selling. Don't waste the tidbits of your time.

Efficiency means getting a higher percentage of result — a better result with less energy.

As you can see, the best way for a traveler to increase his efficiency is to classify his time, so that he doesn't waste his best hours on his smallest jobs, or endanger his best sales by trying to make them at the wrong time.

How to fit the hour to the job, so as to make the best possible use of a day — it is not easy. No. But it is profitable and it can be done.

X
KEEP MENTALLY AND PHYSICALLY FIT

CHAPTER X

KEEP MENTALLY AND PHYSICALLY FIT

Vaccinate Yourself Against Worries — Your Job Is Not a Routine One — It Is All Creative Work

IT is the brain behind the samples that makes the sales. A traveling saleman is not a legger. He is not a coolie, though he often feels as though he were, as he lugs his heavy suitcases about.

He is a brain-worker, much more so than an architect is, as a salesman's brain is in a constant struggle with other brains.

A salesman does not deal with facts, designs, ideas, employees. No. Nothing so easy as that. He deals with other people, over whom he has no control.

His work is very exhausting. He uses up

more energy than most brain workers do. He needs an hour more sleep every night than an ordinary man does.

Isn't it true that many a salesman is all fagged out by Friday afternoon? Isn't it true that he hasn't a kick left in him by Saturday morning. Ask any salesman's wife. She knows.

He eats all sorts of meals. He sleeps in all sorts of beds. He has to deal with all sorts of people. He is all day long in the midst of strangers, fighting a lone battle on behalf of himself and his firm. As you can see, it is very necessary for him to keep fit.

A salesman who stumbles into a busy merchant's office, with a tired body and a jaded brain and fishy eyes, isn't very likely to get an order, is he?

He may try to excuse himself. He may say, "Sorry, Mr. Jones, but I'm a little off color this morning." But what does Jones care? No business man likes to have his office invaded by nervous wrecks.

No. You cannot cut with dull tools. You

Keep Mentally and Physically Fit

must be sharp and well tempered if you want to make money selling goods on commission.

You cannot handle difficult customers if you have a quart of food in your stomach.

You cannot handle him if your brain is crying out for four hours more sleep.

If you sat up until 2 A. M. playing cards, you are about as much use at 10 A. M. as a drunkard.

Thirty or forty years ago, it was customary, in some trades, for the customer and the salesman first to have a carouse together, and then attend to business the next morning. But those days are over. Sales are made to-day by thinking, not drinking.

To-day every ambitious salesman must take care of his health. He must not be ill, nor half-ill, as so many people are.

Appearance counts for a great deal in a salesman. Intelligence counts for more; and both depend in the main upon good health.

I can call to mind a certain traveling salesman for a Chicago house — big, ruddy, smiling — the picture of health! He is welcome wherever he goes. Faces brighten in every room he enters. He has half won his battle before he begins to fight.

Perfect health makes a man almost irresistible. It makes him sway other men as a strong wind sways the branches of the tree.

Good health and good spirits, both! A salesman must be an optimist. It is a large part of his duty to put pluck into timid people — to buck up customers who are faint-hearted.

His head must be clear — as clear as a bell; and his heart must be light — as light as a child's, if he wishes to reach the 100 per cent. mark as a traveling salesman.

He must not be a worrier. He must be vaccinated against worries, else he will not last long on the road.

No other man, in any line of trade, or in any profession, has as many worries as a traveling salesman. He has 3 varieties:

1. PERSONAL WORRIES — created by his own habits, misfortunes or mistakes.

2. BUSINESS WORRIES — created by his company and his customers.

3. Home Worries — created by his wife and children.

As you can see, he has a-plenty. Yet he must carry on — carefree, as though he hadn't a trouble in the world.

That is something that many a Sales Manager, and many a wife, does not think of — the way that worries handicap a traveler and knock his sales down.

If I were the wife of a traveler, I would write him a joyous letter every week — always to reach him on a Thursday, when he is beginning to feel the weight of his job. It would put his sales up 10 per cent. Few wives think of that.

A traveler must keep in fighting trim every week-day, until 6 P. M., anyway. If he wants to over-eat, or over-drink or over-smoke, he should do it after 6 P. M. or on Sunday.

Too much food, drink or tobacco, will slow a man up. It will take the snap out of him. Every athlete knows that, but few salesmen do.

In sport, men know the importance of keeping fit. Ask a jockey. Ask a pugilist. Better still, ask a trainer of athletes and he will tell you that it is no easy matter to keep in the pink of condition.

The wrong sort of a meal may make a jockey lose a race or a pugilist lose a fight.

Often the result of a race or a fight depends upon a fine point of fitness; and so does the result of many an interview, when a salesman is trying to sell goods.

A salesman, in fact, is more of a sportsman than an ordinary man of business. His job is really a game — just as much a game as baseball is.

A sales interview is a battle of wits. It is brain against brain. The better man wins, if conditions are at all normal.

There is no routine work in a salesman's job — that is the big fact to remember.

It is all creative work — combative work, at times. No two customers are alike. A simple parrot-like talk will not do.

The traveling salesman who becomes mechanical ceases to be a salesman. He becomes a mere carrier of samples — quite a different thing.

A traveling salesman has no control over his customers except mental control. He is entirely at the mercy of the customer. He is, in fact, a trespasser if the customer does not wish to see him.

The success of a traveling salesman, as you can see, is largely a matter of personality and intelligence.

A 100 per cent. salesman would be almost a human dynamo. He would be fit — ready in a flash to make good use of anything that happened to him.

A quick answer! How much depends on that in selling goods?

An opportunity that is snapped up in a second! That is the main secret of many a man's success.

Every day is a new day, to a traveling salesman. Every interview is a new adventure. He can no more afford to be careless than a lion-hunter can.

Many a time the result of a sales interview

is decided by the question of sheer vitality. The one that tires first, loses. The sticker wins.

I once knew a keen old business man, who piled up a $30,000,000 fortune; and he would never see anyone on an important business matter unless he was in good form.

"I always drink a cup of coffee," he said, "before I have an important interview with a buyer or a seller. I find it pays me to have my brain as keen as it can be, and not half asleep."

Every traveling salesman would do well to train his mind to notice — to compare — to remember — to create.

There are now plenty of cheap books that will help him to put an edge on his brain. He can develop his memory, too, up to a point.

He can store his mind with all manner of facts, as every sort of fact comes in useful to a salesman.

Customers have hobbies — all sorts of hobbies. One man is keen on music. Another is a

Keep Mentally and Physically Fit 119

lover of birds. Another follows the races. Another was a famous ballplayer in his youth.

If you can meet a man on his hobby you will go far towards securing his permanent good-will.

Selling, from first to last, is a mental process.

So, it is evident that the salesman's brain must not be dull and slow and deadened by narcotics.

It must be tuned up to concert pitch. Or, rather, to change the metaphor, his brain ought to be as quick as a pianist's fingers.

" If I stop practicing for a day," says Paderewski, " I notice it. If I stop for a week, my friends notice it. If I stop for a month, everybody notices it."

That is a great pianist's idea of keeping fit and that is the ideal that I would hold up to every ambitious salesman who wants to make the most of this life.

Keep fit. Keep fit or go into some other vocation that calls for less ability and self-control.

Every day of a traveling salesman's life is a

struggle of personalities. If he is inferior, he loses; if he is superior, he wins. That is the truth, in spite of a hundred sophistries and excuses.

KEEP FIT.

XI

HAVE A STOUT HEART

Chapter XI

HAVE A STOUT HEART

Be a Bit Of a Philosopher — Buck Up Your Customers — A Tip to Wives and Sales Managers

IF a traveling salesman's heart is not stout, it will very soon be broken — that's a truth that every company should bear in mind.

Many a salesman suffers a daily martyrdom for the reason that he has not strengthened himself for his job.

He perseveres, but he shortens his life. He becomes an old man at fifty.

Often, a heartbroken salesman keeps on with his work and trudges about as a mere order-taker. He is no longer a salesman. He is only a spiritless bag-carrier, who walks from door to door and says: " Nothing for me to-day, I suppose?"

The undeniable fact is that a salesman's job is a very lonely and depressing one, unless he takes himself in hand and uses a great deal of self control.

Many salesmen are temperamental. When they are at the top of their form, they could sell the Ten Commandments to a thief; but when they are down and depressed, they couldn't sell fried fish on a Friday.

Ups and downs! Hill-tops and valleys! And the daily average sale, at the end of the year, is very likely surprisingly small.

As anyone can see by a glance in the lobby of any hotel in an evening, many salesmen are in a Slough of Despond. They are bogged. They are discouraged. They are stuck.

This is natural enough. It springs out of the very nature of a salesman's job.

He is away from home for weeks at a stretch He is buffeted about on trains and in hotels.

He is a Robinson Crusoe. He has no co-workers. He is among strangers from Monday morning until Saturday noon.

All the complaints aimed at his company

fall upon him. He does not sit in an office and answer complaints by letter. No such luck. He must go and meet the angry complainer face to face.

He is out on the firing line, not back at the base.

He knows nothing of the pleasures of team-play. He is a lone hunter.

He is constantly facing an indifferent or unfriendly public, and pushing himself in where he is not invited.

He does his work without co-operation from anyone —without sympathy — without applause — often without a word of praise, even when he has done well.

Consequently, almost all salesmen have, at times, fits of depression. Every now and then they are down in the Pit. That is why it is absolutely necessary for every salesman to have a stout heart.

No one can face a dozen rebuffs in a day and keep smiling, unless he is stout-hearted.

These rebuffs do not all come from the customers, either. Some of them come from the home office, and some of them come from his wife.

Letters may make or break a man, so far as his day's work is concerned — home letters especially.

Grumbling, peevish, worrying letter! "You care more for your old firm than you do for me!" "You never think how lonely I am!" "You're having a gay time, while I'm cooped up at home!" And so on.

Pages of self-pity and pathos and petulance! And then the poor chap who gets one of these letters has to go out and face a world of strangers with a cheery smile.

How few wives of travelers realize that the one greatest asset of a salesman is CHEERFULNESS.

The letter that gives a salesman a heartache breaks him down as a salesman. Why don't wives realize that?

To the wives who read this, I would say: "If you are married to a traveling salesman, for Heaven's sake BUCK HIM UP. He has troubles you know nothing about, and unless you cheer him along, HE'LL FAIL and you will be the cause of it. KEEP THE HOME LIGHTS BURNING."

I know one wise salesman who never opens his letters until after lunch. By that time he has had a good start and done half-a-day's work. A man is not as vulnerable, he says, after lunch as he is at breakfast.

There are some Sales Managers who wear spurs. They prick and worry their salesmen. And salesmen have to put up with it, unless it is intolerable. It is a part of the job.

Managers and wives both are apt to forget that a salesman must not have the heart taken out of him, else he cannot sell goods.

A salesman works as he feels, usually. Therefore, he needs praise and encouragement more than anyone else in the company.

He needs cheery letters and good news and a jolly big banquet once a year, with the president of the company in the chair.

Also, he needs to pay attention to his own personal habits, as these often cause fits of depression.

He must not have a sluggish liver and he must have plenty of sleep. He must not lie half awake at night, else he will be half asleep in the daytime.

He must pull himself up if he finds that he is becoming morbid or pessimistic. A Dean or a Professor may be gloomy, but not a salesman.

Timidity, too, is a defect that must be overcome. It is a disastrous drawback, as many a young salesman discovers in his first year on the road.

A rebuff makes him lose his self-confidence for a time. His mind is filled with such thoughts as these:

"I'll leave this man until my next trip — it's too near lunch-time."

"This place is too busy — I'd better not bother them," etc.

All this is a sign of timidity, and no salesman can afford to be timid.

Many a time, in my younger days, I have walked up and down past a door before I had the courage to go in. But that was sheer weakness and nothing else. It had to be overcome.

A salesman cannot be thin-skinned. He must not take offence easily. He must not be a fragile flower.

Once an Irishman was killed at a Kilkenny Fair by a blow on the head. At the trial, it was proved that he had a very thin skull — a "paper skull," as it is called.

The prisoner, in self-defence, said to the Judge: "I put it to your Honor — what right had a man, with a skull like that, to go to the Kilkenny Fair?" The prisoner was acquitted.

So, if a salesman has a thin skin or a thin skull, he has no right to be in the Kilkenny Fair of traveling salesmanship. He is too perishable for such a strenuous profession. He should apply for a gentler job.

A salesman must be a good loser. He must be able to take punishment. In the course of a year, even the ablest salesman will, very likely, take more rebuffs than orders.

That is why a salesman must be a good sportsman. That is why he must take his job as a game, and not as a drudgery.

Win or lose, he must keep on playing. He must not let his company down. I have seen a salesman come into the hotel, as cheerful as a kitten and as bold as a lion, after a day of bad luck. He was a thoroughbred. No squealing. No fainting fits. No glooms. No despair.

The point to remember is that a salesman must carry enough cheerfulness for two — his customer and himself.

Cheerfulness is part of his ammunition — part of his equipment. He needs it as much as he needs his samples.

He must buck up his customers. Many of them are looking at Balance Sheets that would depress anybody. They need to be cheered up.

" My word, Jones, you're like a tonic," said a merchant to a salesman. You may be sure that Jones received an order.

So, a traveler needs to be stout-hearted to sell goods to discouraged dealers. He must have the spirit of Bernhardt.

Her motto was: " In spite of everything." In spite of age — in spite of troubles — in spite of a wooden leg, that indomitable French actress lived her life out to the last second at full speed.

She never slowed down — no, not even for Death. She went — crash — through the barrier.

A fully ripened and matured salesman is always a bit of a philosopher. His nature has grown too large to be troubled by trifles.

He is self-sufficient. He is not like a yacht — blown by the wind. Rather, he is like a liner. He goes forward, wind or no wind, because he carries his own power within him.

As you may have noticed, a young traveling salesman is very much like a peg-top. He must be made to go. Some run for a day and drop and some run for a week. They have to be continually driven forward.

The mature salesman is not like this. He does not become exhausted. He is not a peg-top nor a toy man who has to be wound up once a week.

In a word, he has " guts." He sticks. He takes his job as a daily adventure that is far to be preferred to any safe, stay-at-home, routine job.

Whatever else his job is, it isn't monotonous, thank God. There are never two days alike. And just when he thinks he knows all the bumps, he is apt to find a new one.

Then, at the end of his life — when his last journey has been made and his last order has been taken, he will have a deep satisfaction from his own stoutheartedness. He will say with Henley — " I thank whatever gods there be for my unconquerable soul."

XII

CREATE WELCOMES FOR YOURSELF

Chapter XII

CREATE WELCOMES FOR YOURSELF

Turn Your Customers Into Friends — Keep Your Selling On a Personal Basis

EVERY sales interview should begin and end on a personal note. The customer and the salesman should begin and end as MEN, not as buyer and seller.

This is courtesy and more than courtesy. It is a very important principle of salesmanship that there should be a pleasant finale.

Many salesmen seem to freeze suddenly as soon as the customer stops buying. They begin to think of the next customer or the next train.

Their eyes become dead and their manner becomes formal. Apparently, they seem to be saying to themselves:

"No more orders out of this fellow. Now for the next ordeal."

There may be a formal handshake and a polite good-bye, but if you have suddenly lost interest in people, you may be sure that they are keenly aware of it. They are seldom fooled by formalities. Every woman knows in a flash if your cordialty is real or make-believe; and many men do.

A salesman must always think of his next visit and prepare the way for it. If he does not do this, his visit may have done more harm than good.

He is a welcome-maker. He is an ambassador. His purpose is to create an *Entente Cordiale* between his company and his customer.

A welcome is very important. It saves time, for one thing. It gives the sales interview a running start; and it makes selling easy.

So, whenever a salesman fails to sell, his aim should be to create a welcome, at any rate, so that he will sell goods on his next visit.

Here you can see the reason, too, why a

salesman must not oversell or deceive a customer. If he does, he destroys his welcome.

There are plenty of welcome-killers floating about who call themselves traveling salesmen.

They drift from one employer to another, never remaining long anywhere; and what they cost a firm, no one can tell. But it would be cheaper, usually, to pay such men $100 a week to remain at home rather than to let them run amuck among customers.

All experienced and competent salesmen know that a large part of their work is to create and maintain cordial relations between their company and its customers, as well as to sell goods.

This is so vital a matter that a skilled salesman, when he is working a new territory, will concentrate all his attention upon the creation of welcomes, if his firm will allow him to do so.

A salesman, in a word, must be personally likeable. He must be congenial. If the customer comes to regard him as a pal, all is well.

A certain concern has a Sales Manager who worked up from being a traveling salesman.

He has for years been my ideal of a welcome-maker. He is the sort of man whom you would like to have as a next-door neighbor. His geniality is so sincere that it charms you.

Magnetism? Perhaps. Love for other people — more likely. This attractiveness or congeniality — whatever we may call it — is one of the most valuable attributes that a salesman can possess.

It is a curious fact that few technical men — chemists, engineers, specialists — possess this power of attracting people. That is why they so seldom succeed as salesmen.

They rely wholly upon facts and figures and technical knowledge. They ignore or despise feelings. They are seldom companionable. That is why, if I were selling engines, I would not select engineers as salesmen, but rather men who are skilled in salesmanship.

First and foremost, salesmanship means handling men, not machines. It means winning men over to the point of view of buying your goods.

Few technical men can understand this.

They treat all customers alike; and they have an underlying contempt, which some of them do not conceal, for the ignorance of their customer.

The fact is that a salesman's best asset is the goodwill of his customers. In this matter he is just like a company. I dare say that the goodwill of the Cunard Company, for instance, is worth more than a dozen of its best ships.

The goodwill of the Bank of England — what an enormous amount of money this must be worth! It is almost beyond anyone's power to tell exactly how much this would be.

So it is with the salesman. If he has built up a reputation for honesty, courtesy, knowledge of his goods, reliability, and so forth, he has acquired a real personal capital. Best of all, no one can take this from him. No thief can run away with it. NO ONE CAN DESTROY IT BUT HIMSELF.

" Glad to see you again. I was just expecting you. Come along in." That is the sort of welcome that stamps a salesman as being a professional and not an amateur.

How many welcomes did he make last year? Is that **not one of** the best tests of his efficiency?

How few customers did he lose? What was his net gain in customers?

Can he say: " What I have, I hold "? Has he kept all his welcomes in good order, and has he added to the number?

Isn't it true that every skilled traveling salesman, as he reaches the end of his life, always measures his success by the number and quality of his friends?

Isn't it true that the measure of every man's success is the number of honest people who respect him and believe in him?

MAKE FRIENDS — that is the secret of good management and good salesmanship both.

MAKE FRIENDS — that is how to make any business succeed. Help other people, especially when they are in danger or in trouble.

Don't look on your customers as an orchard of apple trees or as a hive of bees. Don't regard them as the owners of something that you want.

Rather, look on other men as your pals and partners — as the friends who make your business pleasant as well as profitable.

MAKE FRIENDS AND YOUR SALES WILL TAKE CARE OF THEMSELVES. CREATE WELCOMES, AND YOU WILL NEVER LACK ORDERS.

The aim of every company is permanent patrons, not people who buy once and never again. The first sale to a man is seldom profitable. It is his continued patronage that counts.

New customers are costly. They have to be found either by advertising or by canvassing.

Moreover, an established concern is not like a street peddler, who sells continually to new people. A peddler can sell trash. He usually does. That is why he is obliged to keep moving.

But an established concern sells itself with its goods. It will be in the same place to-morrow — next year — in 40 years. It sells to you and your children and your children's children.

A big corporation does not consider the profit on every sale as much as it considers the permanence of its customers.

It regards its customers as its real capital. A customer who buys $2,500 worth of goods a year, for instance, is worth at least $5,000. Why? Because the net profit on $2,500 is about $250, which is the interest at 5 per cent. on $5,000.

To lose such a customer is precisely the same as losing $5,000 out of the bank — how few salesmen realize that?

That is why a salesman must always remember to create a welcome for his next visit. He must make sure that he has not done anything to push the customer away from his company.

All big corporations tend to become bureaucracies. This is bad enough in a factory, and it is fatal to a selling staff.

Traveling salesmen must never become mechanical. If they do, they cease to be profit-

Create Welcomes for Yourself 143

able. Sales letters can be used instead and boxes of samples can be sent to dealers. If nothing is to be done except to show samples, and take orders, there are cheaper ways than by employing salesmen.

The selling of goods must always be kept on a personal basis, no matter how large the company is.

As soon as a customer feels that a manufacturer or wholesaler cares nothing for him he is apt to cut loose and buy elsewhere.

Customers refuse to be turned into numbers and handled like things. Almost all large firms forget this fact of human nature.

A one-man business, handled in a personal way, can always make more profits than a big amalgamation, where there is nothing but system and routine.

Andrew Carnegie, for instance, who treated all his customers as personal friends, made 40 per cent. dividends, while the big Steel Corporation has never made as much, not even in its best year.

People must be treated as people — that is

the last word on the subject. Customers above all! This is the apex of salesmanship.

Every true salesman makes a hobby of people. He studies human nature — the most fascinating subject in the world.

He has no hostility in his heart towards customers. He loves his fellow-beings. He keeps in touch with children and with old people as well. The whole octave of human nature — the whole range of feelings and thoughts and actions — are the constant delight of a salesman who has mastered the complete art of salesmanship.

THE HUMAN TOUCH! That is above all else. All trade and commerce, in the last analysis, is a matter of man to man. Keep human, and you will always have a welcome. And the man who is welcomed is the man who will win, in any of the rivalries of business.

Tips on Leadership

Life Stories of
Twenty-five Leaders

by
Herbert N. Casson

B. C. FORBES PUBLISHING CO.
120 FIFTH AVENUE, NEW YORK

COPYRIGHT, 1927, BY
B. C. FORBES PUBLISHING COMPANY

PRINTED IN THE UNITED STATES OF AMERICA

THE BOOK AND ITS AUTHOR
By B. C. FORBES

Americans have a praiseworthy ambition to become leaders. Energetic exercise of this spirit has been responsible in large measure for the front-rank place America and Americans occupy in the world to-day. The purpose of this book is to present practical pointers on how to win leadership.

Part I is devoted to principles; Part II to personalities — terse, brilliant analyses of how twenty-five outstanding leaders earned their way to the top.

The author, Herbert N. Casson, admittedly is the ablest writer on business and business men in the whole of Britain. Extensive experience in the United States enriched him with a thorough understanding of American business and American business men. He is no dreamy theorist. He is the foremost trainer of business staffs in Britain. He has built up a successful business of his own. Having attained leadership, he, therefore, knows how it is done.

And you need read only a few pages to discover that he can tell in a gripping, fascinating way how you can lead effectively.

CONTENTS

PART ONE

CHAPTER		PAGE
I.	Make Decisions Quickly	3
II.	Be Independent	8
III.	Act And Stand Firm	13
IV.	Always Have A Fight On	18
V.	Learn To Make News	23
VI.	Consider Defeats As Lessons	28
VII.	Form Alliances With Other Leaders	33
VIII.	Walk Towards Danger	38
IX.	Create A Staff	44
X.	Represent Your Followers	49
XI.	Reward Loyalty	54
XII.	Have A Great, Worthy Purpose	60

PART TWO

Edward Wentworth Beatty	67
Luther Burbank	71
Richard Burbidge	77
The Cadbury Brothers	83
Andrew Carnegie	87
Cyrus H. K. Curtis	94
Thomas A. Edison	101
Michael Faraday	106
Joseph Fels	111
Henry Ford	118

CONTENTS

	PAGE
King C. Gillette	125
Warren Hastings	131
Elias Howe	137
Thomas Henry Huxley	143
George F. Johnson	149
Isaac Newton	157
William Pitt	163
Cecil Rhodes	169
Lord Rhondda	176
Charles Seabrook	181
Fred Selous	187
Sir Swire Smith	193
Frederick Winslow Taylor	198
James Watt	209
George Westinghouse	216

PART ONE
Tips on Leadership

Chapter I

MAKE DECISIONS QUICKLY

PEOPLE HAVE CONFIDENCE IN A MAN WHO
MAKES UP HIS MIND IN A FLASH

LEADERSHIP is a thing by itself. It calls for more than ability. It has a Technique of its own.

In other words, it can be acquired to a large extent. It can be learned, as any other Art is learned. And it is the Art that stands highest of all.

DECIDE QUICKLY — that is Tip No. 1.

A Leader must be like a Referee — he must decide in a flash. The Referee's decision may be wrong — no matter. He cannot always be right. But he must always be quick, or he will not continue to be a Referee.

Quickness is not wisdom, but it is a great advantage. Many a race is won by a quick start.

People have more confidence in a man who makes up his mind in a flash than they have in a man who deliberates. They are afraid that the deliberator will change his mind when he thinks of another idea.

A Leader must reflect. He must plan. He must think. But he must not be like Rodin's Thinker — sitting still and absorbed in his own reflections.

When an emergency comes, a Leader must take charge. He must give orders. He must not sit and consider.

Always it has been an emergency or a danger that has created our great Leaders.

While others wondered — looked — feared — hoped — wished, the real Leader told people what to do.

A Leader is never one of these Pro and Con men, such as are often manufactured by universities.

A Leader never says — "Maybe" nor "Perhaps" nor "Possibly I may" nor any other of the noncommittal phrases that most of us use every day.

He never shifts the burden of decision on a Committee nor a Conference nor a Commission.

He knows that the duty of a Leader is to lead and not to draw his pay for nothing.

Why have a President if a Committee is to do his work?

If the rank and file say — "Our Leader doesn't know his own mind," at that moment they cease to respect him.

If a Leader is the prey of the last speaker — if he is pulled about from right to left, and left to right, then he ceases to be a Leader at all. He is only a formality. He inspires no loyalty and he gives no guidance.

A Leader must know what is to be done. He must instruct others and not go about, like a beggar with a hat, collecting the opinions of others.

These opinion-collectors! The political world is full of them; and there are too many in the world of trade and finance.

A true Leader asks advice, when he has time to think; but he never asks advice in a crisis. *He acts.* That is what a Leader is for.

A Leader, in a word, is a man of WILL. He may not be cleverer than the people whom he leads; but he must have the strongest Will.

He need not have the best forehead, but he must have the best jaw. He must have a jaw like a steel trap.

He must say "No" and not "Quite possibly." He must say "Yes" and not "If nothing occurs to prevent."

What he takes up, he must hold fast to and carry through.

Go and look at the desk of many a business manager and you will see piles of half-considered papers— matters in abeyance— matters on which he has made no decision.

His desk is clogged up with this sort of impedimenta. And when he dies, the whole heap of it will go into the waste basket.

Matters in abeyance! Why? Because he cannot decide quickly and either get a thing done or leave it alone.

Here you have one of the commonest reasons why companies and nations fail— they have Leaders who cannot DECIDE.

Above all else, in times of stress, a Leader must be a Decider. He must be in command.

He must stand out, clear and strong, above his rank and file, as a Captain stands out above his crew.

He must be arbitrary— yes, as arbitrary as a Referee in the face of a hostile crowd.

He must be hard— yes, as hard as a Colonel on the field of battle.

He must be fair— yes, as fair as a Judge on the bench in a case of life and death.

But he must stand fast, whether others think

he is right or not. He must not give a fig for others, when a fight is on.

He Must be Loyal to His Own Judgment. That is what will bring him to the top as a Leader.

So, our first Tip is — **Decide Quickly.** There is a speed element in Leadership.

Life is short. One decision leads upwards to another. There are 10,000 decisions to be made.

Decide Quickly.

Chapter II

BE INDEPENDENT

RESPECT THE OPINIONS OF OTHERS BUT MAKE UP YOUR OWN MIND

A LEADER must be a MAN amongst men. He must be the Chief, not "The first among equals" nor any such thing.

But he must be an accessible and a teachable Chief. He must not hold himself aloof, as though, like Moses, he received his wisdom from Heaven.

He must come down from his Sinai of egotism and live among the people whom he leads.

Any one may teach any one something. Napoleon made it a practice to talk frequently with his private soldiers. He listened to every one, but agreed with no one.

Truth, you see, is a composite thing. No one, by himself, can manufacture much of it. Truth is the honey in a thousand flowers. It must be gathered.

No man, however superior in mind, can create his own truth. He cannot secrete it as an oyster secretes a pearl.

Truth is partly created and mostly learned — perhaps that is a better way to say it.

We must gather the raw materials from everywhere and build our structure of Truth, according to our own plans and preferences.

The man who builds his Truth without first gathering materials — he is the man whom we call a theorist.

He builds only on paper. His Truth is not substantial. He is only a child, playing with Truth. He can never be a Leader of full-grown men.

A Leader must go about. He must ask questions. He must respect the opinions of others, but that is all. He must always make up his own mind.

He must be Independent — how strange that sounds! He must not be the prey of the last speaker.

He must not be pushed about by factions and majorities. He must not be heckled out of his own beliefs.

At times he must be arbitrary — of course, he must. What is a Leader for?

He must try to be as independent as Cromwell, or George Washington, or Pasteur, or Darwin.

No nation can be self-led — that is the fact, whether it pleases us or not.

In every nation there are a few people who are wiser and more competent than the others; and Democracy consists in the leadership of this Competent Few.

A Leader must be a THINKER — squirm and wiggle as much as you please, you cannot escape this fact.

He may at times be a despot, but at any rate he is never a ninny nor a demagogue.

There must always be ONE-MAN RULE — yes, why should we continue to deceive ourselves, for fear of hurting the feelings of the stupid?

Every firm — every profession — every trade — every nation has climbed up to success by one-man rule — why should we try to fool ourselves that this is not so?

If you want to smash a Corporation, rule it by a Committee.

If you want to smash an Association, rule it by a Board.

If you want to smash a **Nation**, rule it by a crowd of spokesmen.

The history of progress is all a matter of biography.

A nation is known by its best individuals. That is why ancient Greece stands forever at the head of all the countries of the world — it had more great individuals per 1,000 than any other country has ever had.

In these days of votes, every man who wants to be a Leader tries to please, which is a matter that need not concern him at all.

What would happen to a baby if its mother thought only of pleasing it? It would be poisoned in a week — certainly it would.

There are times when a true Leader must drive his followers like a flock of sheep — drive them to safety.

There are times when a Leader must stand in front of a crowd and be run over and trampled upon — yes, that is the risk of all Leadership.

There are times when a Leader must be crucified — surely I need not prove that.

We have had all this rant about equality and self-determination, and it is time that we put an end to it.

Some men are superior to others, and these superior men should be brought to the front in business and politics.

Some men are experts. They have Aptitude plus Experience plus Personality plus Character.

These men are the salt of the earth. Christ pointed this out 2,000 years ago.

These are the men who serve the crowd, but without taking orders from the crowd — who give people what they NEED, certainly not what they WANT.

So, you can now begin to see what a rare thing is Leadership.

Chapter III
ACT AND STAND FIRM

TO ACT AND THEN TO FALTER IS WORSE
THAN NOT TO ACT AT ALL

RABBITS survive by dodging. So, I believe, do politicians. But in writing of the technique of Leadership I am not referring to either politicians or rabbits.

I am writing for those who are now climbing to the top in business, in industry, in the professions, for the men who carry the world on their shoulders.

In the real world of Trade, Commerce, Finance, Science, Journalism, Literature, Art and the Drama, no man can be a Leader unless he trains himself to act and take the consequences.

A man may be successful in finance or business by being an Artful Dodger. In Art, he may become rich and famous by being a fool. But he can never be a Leader.

Leadership and Success are two very different matters. A very low-grade man may become successful in the art of money-making, but no low-grade man can be a Leader, except now and then, by accident, and for a very short time.

Once in a while, a man sneaks up to the "seats of the mighty" and jumps, in a fit of fear and bravado, into some high position; but he is soon found out and chased back into obscurity.

A Leader must be resolute — firm — rock-like. He must take opposition as a matter of course. He must be able to sleep soundly on the night before a battle.

In a word, he must have the temperament to STICK IT, whether he has made a blunder or not.

No Leader can always be right. He makes mistakes; but he must stick it, right or wrong. That may seem a hard saying, but every one who has been in control of large bodies of men knows that it is true.

If it is said of a Leader — "He does not know his own mind," he will soon be a Leader no longer. A Leader must not be led.

Other men may have the privilege of having "second thoughts," but a Leader must have first thoughts only.

If he dodges or hedges, his people will think that he is afraid, and then it is all up with him.

He must say — "What I have said I have

said," and not proceed to nullify his own orders by making amendments.

He must know that there is a point at which talk ceases and action begins. He must know that Conciliation and Arbitration and all those fine things are good only up to a point, and that after that point there must be ACTION.

Too much arbitration and there will be nothing left to arbitrate — there is a fact that we have forgotten.

Talk is a tool. It is not a thing in itself. If it does not lead to action, then why talk at all?

Talk is a hammer to drive nails with; but if we all brandish our hammers in the air, of what value are the hammers?

A Leader must set a limit to talk. He must keep talk in its proper place. He must act and pay the full price of action. Action always costs. It always brings blame as well as praise. You cannot pick blackberries without being scratched.

There is always criticism. There is sometimes ridicule. There may be threats and anonymous letters and alienated friends. But that is all part of the price that a man must pay to be a Leader.

A Leader is a man who stands on a high place, in full view of everyone. He is surrounded by eyes, looking for his weak points.

He must often decide on action that displeases forty of his people out of every hundred; now and then he displeases everybody.

No weak or timid man can be a Leader. The best he can do is to pick out a good Leader and be true to him. He may climb up to be a Captain, but he can never be a General.

Either do as you're told or tell others — that is a good rule. There is no middle way. We must all command those who are less able than we are, and obey those who are more able.

What to Do — that is the test of all Leadership. We must play the game, not argue about the rules.

ACT AND STAND FIRM — that is the third step of the stairway that leads to the top of your trade or your profession.

Act — and stand by your action when the opposition comes. To act and then to falter is worse than not to act at all.

Men will call you stubborn. So you must be. They will call you unreasonable. So you will seem to be. The time comes when you have had enough of reasoning.

You must be like Luther, who nailed his beliefs to the church door, in full view of everyone. He took a hammer and nails and nailed them fast, so that he could not change his mind and mess himself up with a compromise.

"Here I stand," said Luther, "I can do no other. It is not right for a man to violate his conscience."

He acted and stood firm, and he became the religious Leader of his nation.

And so, in small matters as well as those of greater importance, you will find that it is ACTION that makes you strong and worthy of Leadership.

Chapter IV

ALWAYS HAVE A FIGHT ON

THERE MUST BE A BATTLE SPIRIT IN BUSINESS FOR MEN TO ENJOY WORK

IF A man is negative, apologetic, and timid he may be a very good craftsman, he may have ability and even character; but he can never be a Leader — never in this world.

As I am writing of human nature as it is, not as it ought to be, I am compelled to say that all the world loves a fighter.

It is true, and it is greatly to be regretted, that a pacifist has no follower but himself, while a fighter has always an army at his heels.

Whoever would handle large bodies of men must always be engaged in some sort of a contest. He must always have a fight on.

He must be fighting against competitors, or against some obstacle, or waste, or impossibility.

The main problem, you see, in business life is to get your people wideawake.

How to rouse them from their drowsiness — how to brighten their dull eyes — how to make them keen and quick while working — that is the problem that every Manager has to solve.

Men don't like work — never did and never will. But they have loved games and fights for the last million years.

Fighting is bred in our bones. It is a basic thing. It is not a veneer, as most of our social virtues are. It is bed-rock human nature.

So, as it is one of the principles of Efficiency to treat everything according to its nature, you must put into your business the spirit of struggle. You must have a fight or a contest in order to make your people do their best and enjoy it.

A famous playwright once told me that most of his plays were about a race or a rescue. There must always be a villain, he said, in every popular play; and there must be a struggle to win.

Playwrights know this vital fact in human nature. Novelists know it. Politicians know it. But business men do not, with very few exceptions. And the few exceptions are the men at the top.

Andrew Carnegie knew it, for instance. He introduced the spirit of sport into the iron and steel business and became one of the richest men in the world.

The man at the head of the company must be a Chief — the Chief of his tribe. Without this there can be little loyalty or enthusiasm.

No man will do his best for a routine executive who is trying to change everything into clockwork.

No wage-worker ever yet threw up his hat and shouted — "Three cheers for our Board of Directors."

There must be a battle spirit in business, and in saying this I write as a lifelong enemy of war. I have fought militarism for over thirty years, and I believe that the best way to stop war is to bring the battle spirit into trade and commerce.

Men go to war joyfully because they are fed up with the dullness and red tape of business.

They are bored and disgusted with work. That is why they volunteer in millions for a war.

Men will fight. Well, then, let them fight against competitors. Let them fight with advertisements instead of guns and bombs. Let them fight against waste, and high costs, and difficulties, and the indifference of the public.

Let them have their companies and brigades — and their badges and medals — and their music and marching — and their Corporals and Captains — and their Heroes and Memorials.

When we learn how to honor a victorious Salesman or a courageous Foreman, as we honor a soldier with a Distinguished Service Medal, we shall find out for the first time what loyalty can do in business.

How to get men to do their best — that is the problem, always and everywhere, for every sort of Leader. And the answer is — give them hard jobs and cheer them on and reward them when they win.

How can men be loyal to a man who is always on the defensive? How can they follow a man who is dodging and covering up?

The best defense is attack. Strike first. Keep your imitators on the run, as Kipling said, "a year and a half behind."

In nine cases out of ten, when I suggest an aggressive policy to an executive, he says — "Ah, but you have forgotten this difficulty." Then I know that he is a coward, and there is nothing more to be said.

Of course, there is a difficulty. There always is. That's what puts the interest into life. If there were no difficulty there would be no fight and if there were no fight there would be no fun.

This is a glorious world, packed full with impossibilities — that is the right point of view.

One brave concern has adopted as its motto — "It can't be done, but here it is." That concern makes big profits — naturally it does.

So, if you are to be a leader in any line in life, you must be aggressive. You must always have a fight on.

This one great Fact, keenly realized by any man of courage, would develop him into a Leader among his fellows.

Chapter V

LEARN TO MAKE NEWS

NO ONE CAN AFFORD TO IGNORE PUBLIC OPINION OR TO RESIST IT

OF ALL the facts of our civilization, this one stands out above all the others — that for better or worse we are largely what the Press makes us.

The daily paper is our School. It is our Pulpit. It is very nearly our Creator.

The News dominates us. It has taken the place of Church and State.

So, if the news makes us, we may well ask — "Who makes the news?"

The answer — please note it well — is this, the news is made by all those who do interesting and unusual things.

It is made by all sorts of people, wise and foolish, good and bad, who do something that makes them conspicuous.

The Press, in a word, is not a person, nor a thing in itself.

It is the daily gossip and rumor and scandal and circumstance.

The Press is a vast hopper into which people throw anything they please, very nearly.

It is as much a part of the nation as the heart is a part of the human body.

It is Public Opinion, which is more powerful than gold or Governments or the armies of the world.

No one— certainly no one in business life— can afford to ignore Public Opinion or to resist it.

Rockefeller tried to ignore it. He refused to take any interest in the daily Press. He believed that slanders would die out, and that in the end the truth would prevail.

He was mistaken. His company, which is one of the ablest and most honest companies in America, was smashed by Public Opinion into thirty-five fragments.

Not till then did Rockefeller change his mind. To-day he knows better. He sees reporters and allows himself to be photographed. He has even written the story of his life for the world to read.

The Press agent knows what the Press is. He is one of the few people who do. He is one of the few people who *use* the Press, instead of merely accepting it.

The Press agent has made most of our actors

and actresses. He has pulled trades down and put trades up. He has created and elected our political chiefs.

The sporting editor has made our champions the national heroes; the financial editor decides the fate of most flotations and the society editor opens or shuts the door of social prestige to those who try to enter.

But what has this to do with Leadership? Much. In these days of Public Opinion, no Leader can hope to win unless he knows how to guide the gossip of the day — unless he knows how to Make News.

The news creates the Leaders. Consequently, a Leader must concern himself with the news and control it as far as he can.

A Hermit cannot be a Leader. A man who lives in retirement cannot be a powerful influence in shaping a nation's thoughts.

A Leader must always be in full view. He must stand in the limelight on the stage. He cannot have any more privacy than a goldfish. No man can be a Leader and a modest violet.

Oblivion — that is what a Leader must fear above all else.

Praise helps him along and Blame keeps him alive, but Oblivion destroys him.

Friends and enemies — every Leader must have plenty of both. But the people know and don't care — they are the ones who will drag him down.

If a man or a firm puts Dignity above Publicity, down it goes. Have we not hundreds of examples of this?

If a banker or a manufacturer or a statesman tries to lead the public from a private office, they will soon find that they are Generals without armies.

Stay with the crowd and let them know where you are — there is a tip for would-be Leaders.

"Ah, but must I be blatant?" asks a man who has more education than common sense. No, you need not be blatant, but you must make yourself heard. You must not be dumb.

If you have a dread of publicity, then sell out and live in retirement among your roses and rhododendrons and other dumb things.

Retire or join a monastery, but don't try to make yourself believe that you are a man of business or large affairs.

Merit alone is not enough. I wish it were. I find that I have to spend half of my time in producing something and the other half in making a fuss about it.

We are made or broken by what people say — why shouldn't we face this fact?

We must take the world as we find it and then, as far as our strength will go, we must shape it to our own liking.

If you want to be a **Leader**, you must find out how to **Make News**.

Chapter VI

CONSIDER DEFEATS AS LESSONS

FAILURES AND DEFEATS ARE THE STEPS OF THE LADDER TO SUCCESS

THIS is one of the supreme tests of a Leader — how does he take defeat? Does he take it as final, or does he use it as an educational incident?

The business world is a place of conflict — a place of gains and losses — ups and downs. It is not a pleasant, comfortable office, where you sit at a big desk and are smiled at by pretty girls and flattered by executives.

Business warfare is not a mere matter of signing checks and filling in forms. It is a matter of will power and tenacity and resistance.

It is a tragic fact that most men in the business world are BEATEN men — who stay beaten and regard their defeat as a final thing.

The biggest club in the world, I have no doubt, is the "Down and Out Club." You can see the members of it thronging every city in every continent.

Most men are brittle. They are like the

pitcher that goes to the well, hits a stone and is broken in pieces.

Most men start out in life gaily until they hit the first stone. Then they're done for.

They might do very well in a world that is filled with cushions, but they are not of much value in a world that is filled with stone.

Too many men get into business life who should never have left the nursery. They go through life snivelling — "Somebody hit me."

Too many are given an easy start in life. They had rich fathers, perhaps. And they are led to believe that business is mainly a matter of counting your money and spending it.

These fair-weather travelers are demoralized by the first storm. They are terrified by their first defeat. They are usually, after a bad storm, found among the wreckage.

If a man wants to be a Leader he must prove that he does not break under pressure. He must make it clear that he is not a lath painted to look like sturdy iron.

He must not resign under fire. He must not play the part of the fox with the hounds after him.

Many of our ablest business men failed at first. But they carried on.

The fact is, as all full-grown men know, that failures and defeats are unavoidable — they are just as unavoidable in business as they are in sport.

In all pioneer work — in all experimental work — defeats are unavoidable. They are the steps of the ladder up which we climb to success. Even defeats are useful.

All inventors know this. Edison, for instance, makes a habit of trying one thing after another until, by sheer persistence, he finds what he wants. In this way, by thousands of failures, he invented electric light.

Many men of the pioneer type are always spurred on by a defeat, because it proves that their job is a hard one.

Such men make a hobby of doing impossible things. They scorn the easy jobs and the beaten track. They are the explorers and pathfinders. There are a few such men in trade and commerce; and there ought to be more.

The leader of all dogs is the bull-dog. Why? Because he holds on. Once he has his grip, you can't break him off with a red-hot iron.

That is why every man and every dog looks at a bull-dog with a feeling of the most profound respect.

So, in business life, a man must have the tenacity of a bull-dog if he wants to become a Leader of men. He must even have a certain delight in giving blow for blow.

He must accept life as a conflict, and not expect it to be a parade or a pink tea. He must be quick to notice why he was beaten and to use this knowledge in his next fight.

Too often stubbornness is spoken of as though it were a fault. We call a man obstinate, as though obstinacy were not one of the rarest and most creative virtues in the world.

Obstinacy! Would to Heaven we had more of it. Obstinacy plus Teachability — there you have one of the best pairs of virtues any man can have.

Columbus was obstinate when he kept on for days, in spite of the threats and entreaties of his sailors. Watt was obstinate when he kept on making steam engines that wouldn't work for fifteen years, until, at last, he made one that did work.

Unless a man has the hardihood to keep on, in spite of ridicule and opposition, he can never accomplish anything.

A man with a 50 per cent. brain, who keeps on, can beat a man with a 100 per cent. brain who flits away from opposition and seeks for jobs that can be done easily.

The ancient Egyptians, as you may remember, put this idea into the myth of the Phœnix.

The Phœnix was a sacred bird that lived in Arabia. Every 500 years it went to a certain temple in Egypt and burned itself on the altar.

Then, just when every one thought that it was dead, it sprang out of the flames all renewed. It rose from the ashes of its dead self and lived for 500 years longer.

Yes — if you want to be a Leader in a world that is full of obstacles and enemies, you must be a Phœnix. You must outlast defeat.

Chapter VII

FORM ALLIANCES WITH OTHER LEADERS

SHUN FLATTERY. EVERY BIG MAN NEEDS
FEARLESS CRITICISM AND ADVICE

NO ONE but a big man — a fully matured, ripened man — will appreciate how wise this Tip is.

The average strong, competent man thinks — "I am independent. I am on my own. I have my own firm and my own employees. I must concentrate upon my own interests and pay attention to my own affairs."

Quite true — up to a point. Be independent, but don't stand up against the whole world. No matter how strong you are, the world can easily roll over you.

Be self-made — yes. Every worth-while man is. But don't cut yourself off from the joys of friendship.

Have followers — yes. Every leader has. But don't let your followers spoil you.

Don't let your followers make a conceited ass of you, to put it gently. Don't let them keep you in a Fool's Paradise, where you are never told of your mistakes.

Too many strong men, as you know, are solitary — aloof — cocksure — arbitrary — dignified — irascible. Nobody can tell them anything without first putting treacle on it.

It is an amazing fact that I have been impressed with wherever I have lived — almost every Leader has to be approached with the sweetened word of flattery before he will listen to anything that you have to say to him.

Many times, when I was a young man, I rushed into the presence of a Great Man, and told him something he did not know.

In my youthful ignorance, I fancied that he would be pleased. But he was not. After making many of these mistakes I learned to say to every Great Man — "As you, Sir, of all men in the world, know best," etc., etc. That never failed.

Few men are fit for power. Power makes a fool of them. This is a great pity, and it can be prevented.

Too many big business men make the old, old mistake that Napoleon made. They depend altogether upon themselves and their underlings. They make no alliances. THEY HAVE NO PALS.

Sooner or later, every man who has no pals comes a cropper. He finds himself in St. Helena at the end of his life.

The fact is that every man needs the company of his EQUALS every now and then to keep him from becoming a bloated egotist.

That is the basic idea of Rotary Clubs — to associate with your equals — with other men, in other lines, who are as big as you are.

It is a very important thing for every man to keep his neck straight — to neither swank nor cringe. And he can only do this, usually, in the presence of his equals.

As soon as a man becomes a Leader he must have a Staff of Advisers, but he should not let his Staff degenerate into a mere clique of flatterers and courtiers.

It is quite true, as every one of us knows, that there are hundreds of executives who are paid big salaries for saying, "Yes! Yes!"

They praise every foolish scheme that their President suggests. They cater to his vanity. It may be, perhaps, the only way that they can hold their jobs; but it is a bad thing for a concern when it is run by a King and courtiers.

If you have the power that comes with wealth, get rid of your hangers-on.

If you have the advantage of being married, be thankful when your wife administers a lotion to cure swelled heads.

If you have a son old enough to say — "Dad, you're wrong," then thank God for it and listen to the lad. There's at least one chance in four that he may be right.

If you have any one in your firm who stands erect and looks you in the eye and tells you how something may be improved — ye gods! Promote that man. Double his pay. He is worth his weight in platinum.

As yet, we have no "Society for the Prevention of the Flattery of Great Men." There's no law against flattery, although it ruins more great men than drink does.

Consequently, every man who is a Leader must protect himself from this danger; and the one best way to do this is to make alliances with other Leaders.

Study other Leaders. Read their biographies. This will deeply impress your mind with the fact that you, yourself, are not unique.

One thing every big business man can do — join his Chamber of Commerce and take an active part in its work, without trying to dominate it.

Also, he can always make a friend of his banker. Too often he neglects his banker and makes a pal of his lawyer, which is a very dangerous and costly blunder.

He can make a friend of every one of his best customers, too. Nothing ever pays bigger dividends than that.

The secret of Rockefeller's success was that he was the only oil man, in the early days, who made alliances. He made an alliance with the railways to guarantee them a fixed daily tonnage.

So, as you can see, it is quite possible to be very rich and yet remain simple and sociable.

No big man, in a word, is as big as his job. He needs help. He needs fearless criticism and advice. He needs the stimulation that can come only from other brains that are as clever as his own.

That is why a strong man should not carry his independence too far. That is why he should make alliances with other Leaders in other lines of trade and commerce.

CHAPTER VIII

WALK TOWARDS DANGER

"SAFETY FIRST" IS NOT THE MOTTO OF
LEADERS. PROFIT IS ACCORDING TO
THE RISK

AMONG wild animals, wherever there is any sudden danger, the leader of the herd walks toward it. If he did not, he would no longer be the leader. No herd would follow him.

That is the price of leadership. It is a fair price, and every leader must pay it.

The fact is as true among people as it is among buffaloes. The man who would be a Leader must face danger. He must stand between the danger and the people whom he is leading.

If you take the human race as a whole you will find that cowardice is almost universal.

The great mass of men and women are like rabbits. They dodge and hide at the sight of any danger.

Look at Russia — a herd of 160,000,000 frightened people, dominated by a few hundred

Bolshevists, whose one virtue appears to be courage.

Look at China — a herd of 300,000,000 frightened people, chased about by a few courageous bandits.

One brave man may go either to Russia or China and make himself the Leader of 1,000,000 people.

Russia and China breed very few Leaders. They breed followers only. Russia has had only one Peter the Great. China has had none.

The mass of mankind seek first of all for safety. The first homes were mere hiding-places — caves hidden behind rocks.

"Safety First" has been the motto of the human race for half a million years; but it has never been the motto of the Leaders.

A Leader must face danger. He must take the risk and the blame, and the brunt of the storm. He must be a sort of human fortress.

Either in war or in business life, a Leader must be a man of quiet courage — not a swashbuckler nor a dodger.

The fact is that, to certain people, there is a thrill and a fascination in danger. They are danger-hunters.

Two of the bravest men I know are quiet,

gentle men who prefer danger to aught else in the world. One of them is an aviator who flies to all parts of the world; and the other is a plant-hunter who goes to the most inaccessible and dangerous parts of the earth to bring home new flowers.

Danger is an everyday fact to those who live in the wild parts of the globe. It is taken for granted, like storms and disease.

As my own childhood was spent in the Canadian wilderness, I remember very well that no one was ever safe. There was always danger. No one was surprised when a man was shot, or drowned, or killed by a falling tree.

If you want to get on you must take chances. If you want to be dead sure you might as well stay abed in this world of sixes and sevens.

Nearly every risk is an opportunity as well. It is an opportunity to be a Leader in your trade or profession.

Risks weed out the weaklings. They test us. They separate the few from the many. No efficient man should quarrel with risks.

The profit in business is according to the risk. You can make six per cent. without risk, but not more. All the big prizes are given to the men who faced danger.

That jolly old firm — Lloyd's — make their enormous profits by buying risks from other people. They are dealers in danger, and they have outlived more than seven generations of pessimists.

So you see courage is a virtue in business and finance as well as in war. Always the leading banker in every nation is the one who has the most courage.

Take J. P. Morgan, for instance — the strongest banker that the United States ever produced. He was great, not because of his business ability. He always paid too high a price when he bought. But he had courage and character; and for thirty years he was the leader of the herd in Wall Street.

The point for practical men to remember is that you cannot escape danger; the best way to avoid it is to meet it.

You must learn to take danger for granted as hunters do in the African jungle. They go to sleep while lions roar a hundred yards away.

Self-preservation is a virtue up to a point. You may carry it too far.

What about protecting others? Has not every strong man a protective instinct as well as an instinct of self-preservation?

Must not every true Leader protect his people as a mother protects her child? Must not every large-minded merchant protect his customers?

Must not every successful employer protect his wage-workers?

Is it not the tragedy of employership that workers were obliged to organize themselves against their best friend — the man whose capital gave them a chance to earn a better living?

Without courage no man, however able, can be a leader; and courage can be developed. It was developed by thousands of men in the war. Why not in business?

Often courage can be developed by a sudden effort of Will. A man faces the danger that terrifies him, and, presto — there is a chemical change in him.

In business a man becomes courageous by taking risks and carrying responsibilities. He stakes his money on an idea. He bets on his own abilities.

In every town there is one shop or one factory that is noted for doing things FIRST.

There is always one man — daring and progressive — who puts in the new improvements before his competitors do. His motto is — "I lead — others follow."

He stands out from the great mass of imitators and copyists. When they are going West he suddenly turns and goes North.

Generally he is right. Sometimes he is wrong. But always he proves himself worthy of leadership.

He knows that on the road of progress there is one danger after another; and he knows that the First man to overcome a new danger is the one who gains the most.

Chapter IX
CREATE A STAFF

TO RUN SMOOTHLY A FIRM MUST HAVE AN UNDERSTUDY FOR EVERY JOB

A LEADER is a sort of President, rather than a Dictator. He must have a Cabinet.

Every great firm, to be progressive, must be a one-man business. But the one man must have his Staff of Helpers and Advisers and Managers.

He must not try to run his affairs Alone. If he does he will probably die twenty years the sooner. And he won't build up a permanent business.

No man is too wise to need teaching, nor too strong to need help.

Go back in your own memory and you can call to mind Mr. Know-It-All, whose rule was — "If you want a thing well done, do it yourself."

As you will remember, he died at fifty, and his concern is fast following him to the grave. There are scores of such companies.

A Leader must create a Staff. Just as a Captain of a ship has his First Mate and his

Engineer, so every business man must have his counsellors.

A General has his Colonels. A Colonel has his Captains. A Captain has his Sergeant; and even a Sergeant has his pals. No officer, in an army, is left absolutely on his own.

This is a wise rule, and it can be applied to business as well as to war — every employer and executive should have a small personal group of competent helpers.

Too many business men make the mistake of trying to follow every job through. They take a pride in being indispensable.

Some men will even say — "If I leave my office for a day something is sure to go wrong."

This is a silly sort of self-praise that may be allowed in the family circle, but if it is true it proves that the man who says it is a bad organizer.

It means that his firm is like a hand-barrow, not like an automobile that goes by its own power.

Your skill as an organizer can best be tested by the length of time your concern will run in your absence. If you cannot leave it for more than a week or two, you need to create a Staff.

To run smoothly and without breakdowns,

an organization must have an understudy for every job, from the highest job to the lowest.

No doubt, when Boards of Directors were first invented, they were intended to act as Staffs to the chief executives; but they have now become Tribunals instead. They don't help a president, but they punish him if he fails and reward him if he succeeds.

So we need in every large firm a nucleus of men who are being trained to work better and to work together.

This nucleus is the Staff. It should meet once a week and it should be trained by lectures, books, and magazines.

It should be taught, both by the head of the firm and by outside experts — the more the better.

An employer's first duty, if he wants his firm to grow, is to have a system of Staff Training.

Usually the man at the top wears himself out before his time by trying to act as though he were ten men.

Instead of first educating his Staff as to a new change in his policy, he gives them an order to carry out, which they do not understand themselves.

In a word, every man at the top must work

through others. As soon as you have ten employees, you must have a Staff of one; and as soon as you have 1,000 employees, you must have a Staff of at least 25.

Many a man is good at thinking out large schemes, but he is not good at carrying these into effect. Woolworth, for instance, was a failure until he began to create a Staff.

Even Andrew Carnegie, who was as clever a business man as ever lived, did not carry out his big plans until he found Schwab.

As a Staff Trainer, no one ever did more than Carnegie did. He took 43 young men, all poor, and made them millionaires. What's more, he made them all clever, all except one who went into politics.

As a contrast, compare Carnegie and Stinnes, of Germany. Carnegie believed in a Staff. Stinnes did not.

Carnegie built up a $350,000,000 steel company, thirty-five years ago, and it stands to-day, stronger than ever.

Stinnes built up a $100,000,000 combine in six years, but he did not build up a Staff. He left full power to one of his sons. As a result, the Stinnes Combine is now broken up and the Stinnes episode, in Germany, is a thing of the past.

The Stinnes Combine did not last two years without Stinnes. Why? Because he did not provide for the event of his own death. He did not create a Staff, and all his work was the mere making of sand castles on the seashore.

That is the most dramatic lesson that the business men of this generation have ever had as to the necessity of creating a Staff.

Chapter X

REPRESENT YOUR FOLLOWERS

THE ROAD THAT LEADS TO GREATNESS IS THE ROAD OF SERVICE

WE SHALL now carry still further the idea that a leader must PROTECT those whom he leads.

This is a new idea in the literature of business, and one of tremendous importance.

When you have finished this article, you will see that Leadership is a much higher and nobler thing than most people think it is.

A Leader is not a Dictator. He is not a Bully. He is not a Swanker who struts about and gives orders.

Our idea of a Leader is that of a man who represents and serves those who follow him. We have never clearly defined it in our minds. It is more a matter of feeling than thought, as yet.

My own conception of Leadership, in the business world, is that a company should be like a Scottish Clan.

The members of the Clan are true to their

Chief and he is true to them. If the humblest member of the Clan is injured by an outsider, the Chief comes to the rescue.

The Chief fights for his people. He holds even his life as of less value than the welfare of his Clan.

We have this Clan idea in Science. Why not in Business? We have the Chemistry Clan and the Biology Clan and the Astronomy Clan. Often, the Chiefs of these scientific Clans have given their lives for the progress of the Clan.

Feudalism had many virtues that Capitalism threw away; and now, after a couple of centuries, Capitalism is beginning to appreciate those virtues and to bring them into business life.

Feudalism went down because too many Barons and Clan Leaders thought only of themselves.

That is why Napoleon went down and Charles II and Hugo Stinnes and many other great Careerists. It wasn't Waterloo that smashed Napoleon. It was the retreat from Moscow. It was the discovery that Napoleon was willing to sacrifice half-a-million soldiers to his own personal desires.

That is why so many of our political Careerists fail — they put their personal ambitions first. Then, as soon as the nation discovers this, they are thrown aside.

CAREER VERSUS SERVICE! This is the test that must be applied to all our great men; and those who are Careerists instead of Public Servants must be thrown on the scrap-heap.

Every real Leader gives a service to his people. Take a few examples:

NELSON. Why is he on the highest pedestal in London? Because he lived for England and died for England. He never in his life thought of safety or personal glory or power.

LEVERHULME. Now that he is gone, I may praise him without being called a flatterer. He gave the world better soap at lower prices; and he divided his profits with his working people.

NORTHCLIFFE. He thought, first and foremost, of his readers and of England. He took honors and wealth as tools to work with. He kept on being a reporter, in spite of his millions and his ticket to the House of Lords.

DARWIN. He was our greatest scientist, and he gave us a higher definition of Leadership. He set out to seek the FACTS. He found them and he told them, simply, to the world. He created a higher civilization. He cleared the ghosts and hobgoblins away, and put Reason in place of Tradition.

PASTEUR. Of all Frenchmen who have ever lived, Pasteur is the best beloved. He is the national hero of France. Why? Because his whole life was devoted to the service of his fellowmen.

So, as you can see, if you want to be one of the men at the top, you must give service. Invent a new service for 100,000 people and presto — they will make you their Leader. They will make you rich and eminent.

Here you will see the true idea of Business. It is not profit-snatching. It is not selling $10 worth for $15. It is not getting money from other people.

Nothing of the kind. It is providing a better service at a lower rate for as many people as possible.

The clothier must represent his customers. He must be their buying agent. He must hunt the world to find goods to please the people whom he serves.

The manufacturer must represent the users of his goods. He must think of them when he chooses his materials. He must not make trash.

He must write over the door of his factory —
RELIABILITY.

Here, too, you will see the true idea of democracy, if I may mention this betrashed word among sensible folk.

Democracy means that people shall co-operate, for the general good. It does not mean that people shall be equal in intelligence or rank or political power or wealth.

It means only that every one shall be left free to grow as large as he can, on condition that he does not stunt any one else.

It means that the ablest people shall manage the less able — that the Efficient Few shall be at the top, for the benefit of all.

We may even go further and say that this idea of Leadership is the basis of a true morality as well. It is the pith of Christianity, although this is rarely understood:

"I came not to be ministered unto, but to minister." What is this but my 10th Tip in an older form?

Chapter XI

REWARD LOYALTY

A "LOYALTY CODE" FOR EMPLOYERS

THE longer I live, the more I appreciate Loyalty. It is the cement that fastens a civilization together.

Loyalty was the basic virtue of feudalism; but it was chased out of the business world by Capitalism and Socialism.

It is better than cleverness, because there is no deceit nor trickiness in Loyalty. It is honest. It is reliable. It is the very salt of human nature.

Take the Loyalty out of a man and he rots. He may have great ability, but he is a mere clever devil, whom no one respects.

Look back in your own memory and see what you owe to Loyalty. I can recall three times when my life was saved by loyal friends. So, very likely, can you.

Every one who has lived in the jungle or the wilderness has learned to appreciate Loyalty; but all of us are apt to forget that we need

Loyalty just as much in a city as we do in a jungle.

Loyalty is not a military virtue as many of us believe. It is an everyday, practical business virtue. Loyalty has built organizations up and the lack of it has thrown them down.

Without Loyalty, a company becomes a lot of Slippery Dicks, all trying to fool one another. Every one is looking out for himself.

Actually, I have known some companies where the executives were at war with one another and with the President. All down the line there was a general spirit of suspicion and dislike. How could such companies prosper?

If a President makes himself a sort of sacred Llama — if he hides himself in an inner office and appears to hate the sight of people, how can there be any Loyalty in that concern?

If a manufacturer tells his men that he will make them partners eventually, and if he breaks his word and sells out to a rival, how can there be any Loyalty there?

If an Employer has men and women who have worked loyally for him for twenty years, and if he gives them nothing — no reward, nor diploma, nor any sort of public praise, how can there be any Loyalty in that firm?

Once, while I was visiting a large plant, I saw a woman who had been a faithful worker for twelve years — I saw her paid off and sacked because she ventured to give a sharp answer to the Rajah who was the Manager of the firm. How can there be any Loyalty there?

Are there not some firms that are forever changing their staff? Employees are always coming and going. Why? Because they are not fastened to the firm by Loyalty.

We have been hearing a good deal, in recent years, about labor turnover — the cost of new employees.

We know now that a new employee costs from $50 to $200, what with the training and the loss by bad work and one thing and another.

We know, too, that in an organization where there is no Loyalty, the employees do about half a day's work every day. They are slackers. They have no enthusiasm — no incentive.

So, you can see that Loyalty is necessary and profitable. You can see that it is just as important as Efficiency.

There must be Loyalty, and it must begin at the top. It cannot possibly start of itself among the organization's rank and file.

There is a Law of Retaliation. You get what

you deserve. If you want a crop of Loyalty, you must plant the seeds of it.

The most loyal man I have ever known was not a serf. He was one of the richest men who has ever lived. He was Andrew Carnegie.

Carnegie never forgot a favor. After he became rich, he put down the names of all the people who had ever been kind to him, and he sent them pensions as long as they lived. Some of his pensioners never knew where the money came from.

The stronger you are, the more you must be Loyal. An employer must give honor and praise to every worker who deserves it. He must give gold watches to employees of long service.

An efficient firm must be an organized friendship. It must consist of pals. How few executives know this! How can there be a champion organization without team play? And how can there be team play where there is no Loyalty and friendship?

Make Employees into friends and keep them. Make customers into friends and keep them. Is there any policy more practical than that?

A man's natural friends are those of his own organization and his own town. His fellow-workers and fellow-townsmen! If he is not loyal to them, in Heaven's name, whom can he possibly be loyal to?

Every man who wants to be a Leader must possess at least three Goodwills — the Goodwill of his Customers, his Bankers and his Employees.

This triple Goodwill is worth more to him than money. It is the most valuable thing in the business world.

Men must work together and trust each other — that is a principle of economics that our Universities have overlooked.

This one fact is enough to refute the fallacies of Communism. How can any sort of civilization be built up on envy and jealousy and treachery?

How can men work together and trust each other if they have been taught to believe in class war?

Is it not true that there are two great opposing forces in the world, the Christ-force and the Judas-force? Is not one based on Loyalty and the other on the betrayal of trust? Is not one constructive and the other destructive? And are not these two forces to be found in almost every business?

So, we must develop Loyalty by rewarding it

and by cultivating it in our own natures. To this end I have drawn up the following "LOYALTY CODE":

(1) To pay my debts of gratitude with thanks and goodwill.

(2) To believe no gossip or scandal about my friends.

(3) To appreciate my friends' virtues and forgive their faults.

(4) To promote the interests of my customers.

(5) To do my best for those I work with.

(6) To share my prosperity with those whom I employ.

(7) To be a reliable friend in any time of danger or bereavement.

(8) To be proud of my family, my organization and my race.

(9) To carry my full share of the world's burdens.

(10) To be loyal and true most of all when others fail.

Chapter XII

HAVE A GREAT, WORTHY PURPOSE

PEOPLE WILL NOT FOLLOW A LEADER IF
HE DOES NOT KNOW WHERE HE IS GOING

ISN'T it true that most people are little day-by-day insects, drifting West to-day and East to-morrow?

Are they not ready to go in any direction? Are they not saleable to any one who will pay the price?

Are they not indifferent as to what they do, as long as they can be well paid for it?

Is it not true that many of our so-called Leaders have no purpose — no clear policy? Do they not follow their own mobs about?

A story is told of Lord Rosebery, that when he was a lad at college, he declared that he had three purposes — to marry an heiress, to win the Derby and to be Prime Minister. He succeeded in all of these. In fact, he did more — he won the Derby three times.

The fact is that people will not follow a Leader if they believe he does not know where

HAVE A GREAT, WORTHY PURPOSE

he is going. But a purposeful man will very soon have a number of followers.

A great Purpose broadens, enhances, ennobles a man who possesses it. Walk straight and strongly in a crowded street and other people will get out of your way.

It gives a man the tremendous power of concentration. It turns him into a projectile.

Many a man of very small abilities has become truly great and very powerful by having a worthy Purpose.

Why do we offer prizes to children and to the players in the sports fields? Why do we have a Pennant in baseball? Is it not to give people a purpose — an incentive to do better and work harder?

In salesmanship, do we not have a quota — a high estimate of what we are expected to do next year?

In order to stir people up to do their best, there must always be a crusade of some sort.

That wonderful old tale of Moses — leading his people for forty years through the wilderness, with the lure of the Promised Land! That old tale shall never be forgotten, because it is eternally true of every great Leader — he must point to a Promised Land.

"One increasing Purpose," as Tennyson said — that is what gives superhuman power to a man.

A man who sets out to build a great structure of trade or commerce or finance — a man who has the blueprints of his Purpose to show you — such a man is almost irresistible.

Such a man was Ford, when he set out to build his famous automobile; and Carnegie, when he set out to cheapen steel; and Rockefeller, when he set out to cheapen oil; and Leverhulme, when he set out to give the human race a better soap; and Cunard, when he set out to give people speed and comfort and safety on the sea.

"And all that we said we would do, we have done," said Drake when he came back from one of his expeditions to the South Seas. That is why sailors would follow Drake anywhere. He first said what he would do. Then he did it.

No one needs to be a giant to have a Purpose. Every ambitious man should choose a Purpose to fit his abilities.

Many a small person sets out to do a small thing well, and makes a very fine success in life. There was, for instance, an old peasant woman in Paris, before the war, who knew how to cook

HAVE A GREAT, WORTHY PURPOSE

a duck. Millionaires and Kings went to her little restaurant from all over the world — because she could cook a duck as no one else could.

Every merchant or manufacturer should ask himself — "Am I noted for any sort of excellence or skill or service? Am I doing any one thing better than all my competitors are?"

It is a Purpose that gives enthusiasm — that wakes people up to do their best.

If you have no purpose in particular — if you are just going through the motions and putting in the time between week-ends, then there can be no enthusiasm.

Then there is apathy — the common and almost universal apathy that hangs to most people like a disease.

Apathy means failure — bankruptcy. It is the twin of death. And it is almost everywhere in the business world.

It is the one aim of every true Leader to abolish apathy in his company.

He must show his people what Life really means — keen, vivid, exciting Life. He must put an end to the half-sleep that goes by the name of Life.

He must take the people who are droning

along with a 30 per cent. dilution of Life, and he must bring them up nearer 100 per cent. He who does this to the greatest number of people is a true Leader.

Self-development! There is nothing higher than this. To make yourself grow to your full stature. That is the essence of success and morality and happiness. It is the one way to make the best of this world and every other world.

Why should any ambitious man aim at being a Leader? So that he can live his own life more fully and more freely. So that he can develop his own aptitudes for service to his fellowmen.

Self-development and a great worthy Purpose that benefits others as well as yourself — that is the last word that can be said on Leadership.

PART TWO
Life Stories of Twenty-five Leaders

EDWARD WENTWORTH BEATTY

EDWARD WENTWORTH BEATTY — that is the name of the man who succeeded Lord Shaughnessy as the head of the Canadian Pacific Railway.

To be head of the C. P. R.! What does that mean? There are few other jobs like it in the world, if any. The C. P. R. consists of —

Railway	.	18,500 miles of it.
Telegraph	.	115,000 miles of it.
Steamships	.	400,000 tons.
Hotels	.	$25,000,000.
Land	.	Enough to make several Englands.
Employees	.	100,000.
Total assets	.	Over $1,000,000,000.

Beatty is only forty-nine years old. He was born in the tiny Canadian village of Thorold. His father was an Irish emigrant — an Ulsterman, I believe. His mother was an English girl named Harriet Powell.

He had what is called a good education. His father owned several small steamships and was rich enough to keep young Edward at school until he became a B.A. and a lawyer.

However, he paid less attention to studies than to sports. He was not much of a student of the dead languages and other dead things. He preferred the living to the dead.

He kicked his way to the captaincy of the football team. He was one of the best quarter-backs in Canada, and is to-day very skilful at hand-ball.

When he grew to be a full-fledged lawyer, he did a wise thing — he picked out the biggest, richest client in Canada — the C. P. R. — and became the youngest member of its legal staff.

Then he did another wise thing — he set out to learn more about the C. P. R. than anybody else. He became a real student of real things. He spent his days and nights learning — learning — learning. He became a C. P. R. Encyclopædia.

He was soon so full of C. P. R. information that when any one asked Lord Shaughnessy a difficult question about the railway, he would say — "Go and ask Beatty. He knows."

At twenty-eight young Beatty was made assistant solicitor of the railway. Up he went, until at thirty-six he was chief solicitor.

At this time the C. P. R. was passing through a stormy period. It was the richest and ablest company in Canada, and consequently all the demagogues and Bolsheviks were trying to smash it.

Politicians, like death, love a shining mark, and dozens of them were aiming their darts at the C. P. R. The usual Commission of political hecklers was appointed, and a general attack was made on the railway as though its success had made it a social menace.

In front of the C. P. R., protecting it, stood young Edward Beatty. He was clean-shaven and boyish-looking. Worse still, he was unknown. His name was not in "Who's Who." He was rather undersized, too, and not at all fluent.

At first the Commissioners regarded him as a sort of insult to their dignity. But the investigation began, and presently they found themselves beaten at every point. Beatty refused to retreat an inch. Instead of apologizing, he took the offensive. He overwhelmed them with FACTS.

He was not glib nor smart. He did not split hairs. He reasoned. He explained. He gave the exact figures. HE PUT FACTS AGAINST OPINIONS.

He won, of course, because he applied the scientific method. He fought his opponents with data — irresistible data.

To-day he is at the head of the whole railway, and he is proving to be a great Manager as well as a great lawyer.

So, the secret of Edward Beatty's success is that he is tirelessly digging for facts. He is dogged — thorough — loyal — and always in dead earnest.

He is a constant reader — always has a book or a brief in his pocket. He cares little for society. He is unmarried. He has only one interest — the welfare of the C. P. R.

In appearance he looks like Sir David Beatty. Like Sir David, too, he wears his hat tilted over one ear. He has keen, piercing eyes, that seem to look clear through a man. He is quiet-spoken and modest. He is always thinking of the job, not of himself.

He is a great believer in what he calls "the intensity of life." As he said in an interview:

"To-day it is not the length of your life, but the intensity that counts. The wise man crowds all he can into every minute.

"What I want to do is TO GET AS FAR AS POSSIBLE IN THE SHORTEST POSSIBLE TIME."

LUTHER BURBANK

BURBANK was the plant wizard of California. He created more new flowers and fruits than any other man. He was the King of the Gardeners.

He taught roses to grow without thorns and the cactus to grow without spikes.

He taught potatoes to grow larger and cherries to put their seeds outside.

He educated the Shasta daisy into a great, glorious, pure white flower.

He applied Scientific Management to gardening, with results that astonished the world.

He produced scores of new and better varieties of fruits, flowers, vegetables, shrubs and trees.

He was the Edison of the garden — the highest authority in the world on the soil and its products.

At seventy-seven, when he died, he was a slight, thin, smooth-shaven man, with snow-white hair and kindly eyes.

He was born poor, as most worth-while people are. His father was an English-American who made a bare living on a little stony farm in New England.

Poor little Luther had no money — no health — very little schooling and no advantages of any kind.

He did not think that he was any kind of a genius, and at first he drifted about, trying only to make a frugal living.

He worked in a plough factory for fifty cents a day. Then he took a slightly better job in a furniture shop.

But he soon found that he had no skill in manufacturing or selling. He resolved to be a Doctor and began to study medicine.

Then, when he was twenty-six, he had a sun-stroke which nearly put an end to his life.

Ill and poor and friendless, he went to California. He had no trade. He had no skill. He was a farm-laborer — nothing more.

At first he found no one who would give him any work; and he kept himself from starving by cleaning chicken-houses.

Finally, he was engaged as a helper in a nursery; but his wages were so low that he was compelled to sleep in the hothouse.

This made him ill with a fever and he barely saved his life. In fact, he was saved only by the kindness of a poor woman, who brought him a pint of milk every day for several weeks.

As soon as he was strong enough, he found a better job. He saved most of his pay and bought a little nursery of his own.

Then came his first opportunity — a wealthy fruit-grower offered a large sum of money to any one who could deliver 20,000 young prune trees in ten months.

All the nurserymen said — "Impossible." Not one would undertake such a task — not one except Burbank.

He delivered 19,025 young trees in six months — a record-breaking achievement. He won the prize. Better still, he at once became famous as the ablest nurseryman in California.

His nursery prospered. It became known all over the world as "Burbank's Experimental Farms," Santa Rosa, California.

During the last ten or twelve years of his life rich men helped him a bit; but in his earlier days no one helped him — no one except the poor woman who saved his life.

He was always frail. Twenty-five years ago the doctors told him he had only eighteen months to live. But Burbank only smiled and went off in the mountains for a three-weeks' holiday.

He worked from ten to fourteen hours a day for over forty years. That is how he became a "Wizard."

He never believed in fairies or in luck. The secret of his success, he said, was mainly hard work and persistence.

He developed several new varieties of plums — the Gold, Wickson, Apple, October, America, Chalco, Santa Rosa, Formosa and Climax.

He created new prunes — the Grant, Splendor, Sugar, Standard and Stoneless.

New Roses, too — the Peachblow, Abundance, Burbank and Santa Rosa.

One by one he created new varieties of apples, peaches, nuts, berries, grasses, grains and vegetables.

He originated one fruit that is absolutely new — the Plumcot.

At one time he personally conducted 6,000 experiments. He raised 1,000,000 plants a year for testing purposes.

Although he had very little schooling, he was one of the most distinguished professors at the Leland Stanford University, lecturing on Evolution and Education.

He published the long story of his methods and discoveries in twelve volumes.

He was so absorbed in his work that he did not get married until he was seventy-one years old. His nursery was his home as well as his business.

Burbank was fascinated with plants and their possibilities. He loved to take a weed or a common little plant and develop it into a higher form.

He loved to show Nature a short cut — a quicker way to evolve.

He made his nursery a great University of Gardening. He solved the secret of the education of plants and trees.

Plants, he found, are very much like people. Some are teachable and some are not.

There are certain species of palms, for instance, that cannot be taught anything. They cannot be improved. They are stubbornly opposed to any kind of a higher life.

Burbank had strong views on Education. He did not believe in cramming little kiddies with book knowledge. No child, he said, should be bothered with books until he is at least ten years old. He should be taught first in the nursery, the garden, the fields and the playground.

"It is a crime against Nature," he said, "to

take the tender HUMAN plant and force its mental development prematurely in the hothouse atmosphere of the schoolroom."

Burbank never travelled. He never had time. But wise men from all parts of the world travelled to see him at Santa Rosa.

He had a life of the highest success. He began in a pit of poverty and illness and he climbed to a peak of fame and wealth and national service.

And mind you — nobody helped him — nobody except a poor woman who gave him a few glasses of milk in the name of the Christ.

RICHARD BURBIDGE

IN 1860 a small boy of thirteen, not a very strong boy, got on board a train at a farming village in Wiltshire, England. He rode in a third-class coach, which in those days was open to the weather, and he had bought a ticket for London — eighty miles away.

His father had died a few weeks before. His mother had ten children in a small house. So this little lad was sent as an apprentice to the great city of London.

His mother had paid $500 to a grocer in Oxford Street, to pay for four years' apprenticeship. As for the little lad's wages, he had none. He had only his bed, his food and twelve cents a week.

The boy, on his first holiday, went to see the Crystal Palace. This impressed him beyond words. He was fascinated. He was inspired. That day was the most wonderful day of his life.

Fifty-two years later, when the Crystal Palace was in danger of being torn down by a generation not worthy of it, our greatest English merchant quietly stepped forward and gave $160,000 to save the Crystal Palace for future generations. He gave it in memory of his first holiday, when he was a poor little errand-boy.

His name was SIR RICHARD BURBIDGE.

Little Dick Burbidge was a real Dick Whittington, and far more successful. He became more than a Lord Mayor. He became a LORD MERCHANT, having built up the largest shop in the British Isles.

Dick Burbidge had very little schooling. He had no rich friends. He had no luck, as some men do. He never got something for nothing. He never asked for either a dole or a subsidy.

His only asset, at first, was HIMSELF; and his only advantage was a wonderfully competent mother. His mother taught him to WORK. She made the bread, butter, cheese and bacon for her family of twelve, and did all the washing as well. She, in her own way, was fully as efficient as any of her clever sons.

Young Richard was a natural merchant. When twelve, he would buy five buns for six cents and sell them for two cents each.

As an apprentice, he was a success. He made a lifelong friend of his employer. But he did not waste any time — he started a little grocery shop of his own as soon as he was eighteen.

He carried on in this shop for sixteen years, but all the while he was studying how to operate an immense shop that would be a complete market place for all manner of commodities.

In 1881 he sold out and became manager of the Army and Navy Auxiliary Stores. Soon afterwards he became manager for Whiteley — he was selected out of 400 applicants.

He remained at Whiteley's for nearly nine years; then, in 1890, he went to Harrod's, and set to work to realize the dream of his life.

At that time, Harrod's was a limited company, with a capital of $700,000. Mr. Burbidge built it up until in 1906 its profits were more than $700,000; and in 1924 they were more than treble that.

In 1917 his employees — more than 7,000 of them, held a mass meeting in his honor in the Royal Albert Hall — that was perhaps the proudest moment of his life.

As to the METHODS by which he made his success, they were the usual efficiency methods, as taught by Taylor and others.

Sir Richard knew how to organize — how to plan — how to pick competent men — how to serve the public.

He put his managers on their own, and held

them responsible for results. He freed himself from the details of routine.

His habit was to rise at 5.30, as he had learned to do on the farm. He had a ride on horseback before breakfast. His work at the stores began about 8.30 and continued until 6.30. He arrived home at seven, had supper and a game with his children, and went to bed at 8.30. All his life he was opposed to late hours.

When he was a young man, he wrote out the following eight RULES for himself:

(1) Be persevering.
(2) Be moderate in smoking, drinking, etc.
(3) Be prompt and punctual.
(4) Be courteous.
(5) Don't shift about from one firm to another.
(6) Don't look down on any one.
(7) Don't pester visitors to buy.
(8) Don't fail to make your employers' interests your own.

Although he worked ten hours a day himself, he believed in shorter hours; and he was a leader in establishing the Saturday half-holiday.

He believed in making his shop a place of entertainment. He was always planning new attractions.

He once brought 12,000 people all the way

from Bournemouth to a special sale. He chartered trains and sold cheap tickets.

He put in the first moving stairway.

He started the free delivery of goods to the country.

He introduced shopping by telephone.

He gave his customers a restaurant and a reading-room.

Always something NEW — that was the Burbidge's policy. His shop was always ALIVE. His employees were keen and wide-awake.

Burbidge made war on stupidity and stagnation, and rudeness and oblivion all his life, and HE WON.

He built up the largest and handsomest and best-known shop in the British Isles.

He was fortunate in his marriage; he married "the pretty Miss Woodman," as she was often called, who lived near his home in Wiltshire.

During the War he overdid himself. He was overwhelmed with duties, and he accepted them all.

He sent 3,200 of his young men to the front. He trained girls to take their places. Like many others during the War, he did double work with half a staff.

Then, in 1917, his body broke down under the

strain. "I'm tired," he said to his daughter. He sat in his armchair, and in a moment, quietly, he had passed away.

Sir Richard Burbidge was a great MAN as well as a great merchant. As Mrs. Stuart Menzies says, in her biography of him, "He was a man who never forgot a kindness or an old friend."

Wealth, success and honors he had in plenty; but they did not spoil him. He worked for fifty-seven years, and he died in harness. He bequeathed to his children and his employees THE HERITAGE OF A GREAT LIFE.

THE CADBURY BROTHERS

ALL the world has heard of Cadbury Brothers. There were two of them, Richard and George. Richard has been dead more than twenty years; but George lived until 1922.

There are now 8,500 Cadbury workers and not a Bolshevist among them.

There has never been a strike at Cadbury's — might as well try to have a bonfire underneath the ocean as a strike at Cadbury's.

It is the largest cocoa business in the world. Also, it is an object lesson in employership to the coal and cotton and shipbuilding trades.

I am confident that there is not, either in the United States or Europe, a concern that has done more to develop the art of employership than Cadbury's has.

Talk about Whitley Councils! The Cadburys have had them for fifty years.

Talk about Welfare Work! The Cadburys didn't hire some one to do it for them. They did it themselves.

They visited those who were ill. They played and prayed and labored and consulted with their workers. They were just naturally sympathetic themselves, so that they didn't need to hire any professional sympathizers.

Richard was born in 1835, two years before the first railway ran to Birmingham. George was born in 1839. Their father died at eighty-eight, and was for fifty years a leader in all good causes in Birmingham.

All the Cadburys have been Quakers for 200 years. They have always been pioneers. They fought against slavery and whisky and militarism and oppression of every sort.

They were always Commoners. No peers. No lords. Not even Mr. and Mrs. in the earlier days, just Richard and George and Mary and Elizabeth.

The two brothers started with a tiny works in 1861. For three years they lost money.

But they only worked harder; and in 1864 the tide turned. They made their first profits.

The secret of the Cadburys' success, as it seems to me, is the fact that they combined two good things:

(1) Old-fashioned virtues.
(2) New-fashioned methods.

They were industrious, **punctual**, reliable, **careful**, earnest and kind-hearted.

Also, they were the first to sell sweets in pretty boxes, the first in their line to adopt mechanical accounting, the first to have a complete planning department, and so on.

They moved from Birmington to Bournville in 1879. Why? In order to give their workers better conditions.

"We have thought it over," said one of the Cadburys in his diary, "and we consider that our people spend the greatest part of their lives at their work, and we wish to make it less irksome by surrounding them with pleasant sights, sounds and conditions."

Their aim was to gather together a group of useful, contented people, who would make cocoa and sweets for the public.

Here, at Bournville, they used about half the land for houses and factories, and the other half as a playground. They built the best factory gymnasium in England. They built schools and clubs. They set up a great pipe organ in the girls' dining-room. They built 1,000 cottages for workers and thirty-three pretty little homes for old workers who had no money for rent.

Being fond of sport, they played cricket with their men and bought one of the first bicycles for the boys of the factory.

They were keen on gardening. They gave seeds and bulbs to their workers and planted flowers around the factory.

Both were boyish men. They were fond of children and horses and dogs. They wrote poetry and sang songs. They made their business half a game and half a religion.

They were always simple and human. Every morning they gathered their workers around them, sang a hymn and offered up a short prayer.

They were always get-at-able. They took wealth as an obligation, not a privilege.

Once, when one of them was walking on a Birmingham street, he met a poor woman trying to wheel a barrow of coals. He stopped, and wheeled the barrow home for her. He did it because he felt like doing it.

The Cadburys' always had schools — factory schools and Sunday schools. They were real leaders of labor as well as captains of finance.

And the secret of their success was — don't forget it:

(1) OLD-FASHIONED VIRTUES.
(2) NEW-FASHIONED METHODS.

ANDREW CARNEGIE

IF I were asked — "Who was the most competent, generous, original and independent man in the world?" I would be obliged to answer, "Andrew Carnegie."

He would also have been the richest, if he had not given away $300,000,000.

All through his long life, Carnegie's motto was — MORE. HE MADE more — GAVE AWAY more — DID more, than any one else, with the possible exception of Mr. Rockefeller.

Carnegie was born in Dunfermline, Scotland, in 1835, in a wee cottage. His father was a weaver — poor and discontented — a sort of local labor leader.

When he was a little chap of ten, he saved enough to buy half a box of oranges which he peddled profitably from door to door.

When he was thirteen, lack of work compelled the whole family to go to America. They set sail on a tiny schooner and made the voyage in forty-nine days.

Little Andy at once found a job as bobbin-boy at $1.25 a week. His father went to work in a cotton mill; and his mother took in washing. They lived in a back street which was known as Barefoot Square.

In a few weeks Andy was promoted to be a stoker, at $1.75 a week. A year later he became a telegraph boy at $3 a week.

He had little or no schooling, but he was keen on reading. His eagerness for books attracted the attention of a kindly man named Colonel Anderson, who offered the use of his library to the young Scottish boy.

THAT LIBRARY WAS THE MAKING OF CARNEGIE. It developed him from an errand-boy into a leader of men.

When he was seventeen, he had taught himself telegraphy. One day when the operators were absent an important message came in, and he jumped to the instrument and took it. This was against the rules, but he was promoted at once to be an operator at $6 a week.

Two years later, he jumped in again and cleared up a railway accident. This was also against the rules, but he was promoted to be the secretary of a railway manager.

He saved his money and bought shares in all sorts of companies. For ten years he was a clerk — an assistant to the head of the railway.

He was full of initiative. While others deliberated, he acted. When the Prince of Wales visited Pittsburgh, for instance, young Carnegie jumped forward and said to the Prince — "Would you like a ride on the engine?" So the future King of England and the future King of Steel had a gay ride together in the cab with the engine-driver.

At twenty-seven, Carnegie made his first $1,000 in an oil venture. He made more by backing the Pullman Company, which originated sleeping-carriages on railways.

Then, when he was twenty-nine, he bought a one-sixth interest in a little iron company for $9,000.

It was a miserable little iron company. It paid no dividends. It wobbled about on the verge of bankruptcy.

The other shareholders lost hope, so Carnegie bought them out. He hung on. "What we need," he said, "IS MORE BUSINESS." So he gave up his railway job and became a salesman of iron products.

He got larger orders at better prices. He put in better machinery. He worked like a demon. Very soon he became what most of us would call rich. But he wasn't satisfied. He wanted MORE.

At thirty-one he visited England and saw a steel rail at Derby. At Sheffield he saw a Bessemer converter for the first time, and it fascinated him.

He rushed back to America and built a Bessemer steel works. He borrowed from everybody he knew. He staked all he had on steel.

In 1881 he had become the greatest steel-maker in the world. He had 45,000 workers.

By 1889 he was willing to sell out, and offered his company to his own partners for $155,000,000. They were not quick enough, so Carnegie offered it to Rockefeller for $250,000,000.

Rockefeller said, "Too much"; so Carnegie started a selling campaign. Once again his motto was "MORE."

He made war on his competitors until they decided to buy him out at any cost. They paid him $450,000,000 in bonds and shares.

At once he became the richest man in the world. He had a pension of $15,000,000 a year. "Hurrah," he said, "I'm out of business."

In general his policy as a business man was as follows: —

(1) Mass production.
(2) The most improved machinery.
(3) Concentration. "Put all your eggs in one

basket," he said, "and watch that basket."

(4) Avoidance of details. He usually managed his business from a distance.
(5) Travel. He believed in keeping in touch with outside influences.
(6) Daily reports from all managers.
(7) Giving managers small salaries and large commissions, payable in stock.
(8) Reinvestment of profits in the business.
(9) Appreciation of chemistry and machinery.
(10) High wages, high profits and low costs.

In his philanthropy, too, Carnegie always had one fixed policy — help the man who is trying to help himself. He never gave anything to help the "submerged." He did not believe in, charity, in the ordinary sense.

He built 3,000 libraries, so that people can read books, as he did, and improve themselves. On these libraries he spent $60,000,000.

No wiser or nobler act was ever done than this — the opening of the doors of knowledge to millions of people in all English-speaking lands.

He gave $50,000,000 to scientific research; and $25,000,000 to Technical Schools, and $10,000,000 to the Scottish Universities.

He built the Temple of Peace at the Hague —

a snow-white building which the world has not deserved.

His only extravagance was travel; and he always regarded travel as a business necessity.

He had the simplest of tastes. He was a feather-weight man, only five feet four inches high. He weighed no more than four feet of steel rail.

From the first, he always regarded business as a game. He never let his money master him, as most of us do.

He was a boy-hearted man, always keen, enthusiastic and quick to act. His brain was always bubbling over with new ideas for the improvement of the human race.

He had far less dignity than the average clerk. I have seen him squatting on the floor of his library, in his New York home, arranging charts and papers on the floor.

He didn't care a ha'penny for looks. He wanted to play the game and win.

His hobbies were steel; libraries; peace; democracy; and — to a certain extent — science and music.

He had a passion for books. Once he said — "If I had my life to live over again, I would prefer to be a librarian."

He detested starched clothes and fashionable society. He avoided the society of the rich. He married when he was fifty-two, and his wife devoted herself to housekeeping. They had one daughter — a delicate girl who, at twenty-two, married a young American railway manager. Carnegie would have been heartbroken if she had married a Duke.

He was a good employer — always first to raise wages. He was not to blame for the Homestead strike. He never economized by cutting down the pay of his workers, but by improving the machinery.

He made tons of money, but it was all clean money. He made nobody poorer. He earned it, as the fee of leadership. When he was born, steel was twenty-five cents a pound. He reduced it to one-and-a-half cents.

He was a capitalist; and his career is a complete answer to Bolshevism. He robbed no one. He raised wages. He made the work easier. He made more jobs. He lowered prices. He built up a great trade for the benefit of the whole world.

And he began life in a wee cottage in Dunfermline. Such is the Epic of Carnegie — the greatest of all industrial Scots.

CYRUS H. K. CURTIS

THIS is the story of a man who began with three cents and who now has a capital of many millions.

It is the story of the man who has done most to lift up the standard of quality in both JOURNALISM and ADVERTISING.

He is now seventy-six years of age. His name is CYRUS H. K. CURTIS. He is the owner of the *Saturday Evening Post, Ladies' Home Journal, Country Gentleman, Philadelphia Public Ledger* and *New York Evening Post*.

His *Saturday Evening Post* sells at five cents and has a circulation of more than 2,600,000 a week.

His *Ladies' Home Journal* has a circulation of over 2,000,000 a month, at ten cents.

His income from advertising alone is now about $65,000,000 a year. And not a penny from whisky or cure-alls or any sort of catchpenny rubbish.

He is the most successful publisher in the world, and there is no scandal in his reading matter, and no humbug in his advertisements.

His father was a decorator, who lived in a small wooden house in Portland, Maine, and he was born in 1850.

One day, when he was twelve, he asked his mother for some money to spend on firecrackers. "If you want money," she said, "you must go and earn it."

He had three cents in his pocket. He went and bought three *Daily Couriers* and sold them on the street-corner. At the end of the day he had nine cents. He was a tiny lad, quick but not strong; but he soon became a very competent newsboy.

When he had been selling papers for a month he had his first business idea. He ran in to the Manager of the *Courier* and asked for credit. "If you give me credit till to-morrow morning," he said eagerly, "I'll take a big bundle of *Couriers* across the river to Fort Preble."

The Manager agreed. Then young Cyrus arranged to get his papers first and to slip out of a side door. He went to Fort Preble and made a new market for the *Courier*. Soon he was making a profit of $2.50 a week, which was half a man's pay in those days.

The next year, when he was thirteen, he started a little paper of his own. It was a four-page boys' paper, called "*Young America*"; and it had a net sale of 100 a week. He had bought a hand-press for $3 and he was doing well, when a fire burned him out. No insurance. "*Young America*" went up in smoke.

Then, for six years he worked in a drapery shop. During this time he did nothing remarkable and was probably not aware of his own nature and abilities.

At twenty he went back to the Press. He was given a job canvassing for advertisements for a half-dead paper in Boston. One day the discouraged owner offered to sell him the paper for $250. Curtis refused. "All right, then," said the owner, "you can have it for NOTHING."

Curtis took it and for the next five years he wished he hadn't. It was hopeless. At twenty-five he chucked it up, got married and went to Philadelphia.

It was his marriage that brought him his first success. He had started another paper — the *Tribune* — and one day his wife called his attention to the so-called "WOMAN'S PAGE." "Who wrote that?" she asked. "I did," replied Curtis. "It's utterly ridiculous," she said.

"Well," said the wise Curtis, "perhaps it is. Will you write a page for me?"

She did. Her page at once became the best part of the paper. Soon it became the WHOLE paper, and it was called the *Ladies' Home Journal*. To-day it has a circulation of 2,000,000 and is the leader of all women's magazines.

Curtis soon found that his business had grown too fast for his capital. He needed far more than the banks would give him.

The man who came to his assistance was N. W. Ayer, an advertising agent. Ayer was the first man who fully appreciated Curtis. He not only lent him $250,000, but gave his note to a paper-mill for $125,000 more.

In eighteen months Curtis had paid the whole amount back; and the N. W. Ayer Company is now the largest and richest advertising firm in the world.

One of the secrets of the success of Mr. Curtis is that he never wastes time messing and fussing with what he has already got. His policy is to go and get something else. HE LETS HIS SUCCESSES ALONE.

So, as soon as the *Ladies' Home Journal* was a success, he went out and bought a little weekly called the *Saturday Evening Post*. It had been founded by Benjamin Franklin, but it had no other assets of any account. Curtis bought it for $1,000. It was dead and buried, but Curtis is a great believer in resurrection.

Everybody made fun of him for buying a paper that had nothing but a name. But Curtis had a NEW IDEA. In 1897, he was fascinated by a book, called "CALUMET K," written by a newspaper man. This book was a romance of business. It opened his eyes. It showed him that BUSINESS is the most interesting as well as the most useful of all the activities of the world. He dedicated his new magazine to BUSINESS.

At first, it didn't go. He lost money on it. He nearly lost ALL his money. He lost $1,500,000 on it before it started to go up.

To-day it is the most profitable publication in the world. It stands in a class by itself. It charges $8,000 a page. It refuses one half of the advertising that is offered to it.

In a single issue, it has carried $1,000,000 of advertising.

Next, he bought a poor but proud little paper called the *Country Gentleman*. It was long on pedigree but short on subscribers. He worked at it till he had a circulation of 600,000 a week.

Then he went out and bought the *Public Ledger*, which also was both historic and anæmic.

The real reason why he bought the *Ledger*, I

believe, is because when he was visiting London, some one gave him a "LIFE OF JOHN DELANE." Delane was the greatest of all the editors of *The Times*. He was independent. He was "THE THUNDERER."

The story of his life deeply impressed Curtis. He bought a copy of the book for every editor and reporter in his employ.

He has built up the *Ledger* until to-day it is sold in every city in America. More recently he bought the *New York Evening Post* and is infusing new life into it.

Physically, Mr. Curtis is small, with kindly eyes and quiet manners. He wears an old-fashioned beard, cut short and squared.

He is a man who cannot be classified. He is both old and young. He is equally Capital and Labor. He belongs to none of the silly castes that divide one man from another.

He takes life seriously, but he runs away from pomp and ceremony. If he goes to a meeting, he takes a seat at the back. He is as simple and human as his father was.

To his friends, he is a lovable man and full of surprises. Several years ago I had the good fortune to sit beside him at several banquets. He and I were co-speakers at the American

Luncheon Club, too; and I found him full of the joy of life. He is wonderfully balanced and wise.

He is a gentle-man, in the highest sense. He never bullies nor swaggers.

As to his habits, he works, jokes, smokes, dances, reads, travels, plays the organ and goes to church. He is fond of yachting. He loves children.

When he has a hard problem to solve, he plays solitaire, as Theodore N. Vail always did.

He leaves detail alone, as soon as a right routine is established. His main business, he thinks, is to make suggestions for improvements and to start new lines of work.

He is non-political.

He never forgets a kindness. Long ago, when he had a poverty-stricken little paper, a Scottish printer named Allan helped him and refused to take pay for it. Twenty years after, Curtis heard that Allan was in need in a distant city. At once he went and found him, 1,500 miles away, living in a garret. Curtis gave him a cheque that banished all his money troubles for the rest of his life.

THOMAS A. EDISON

EDISON is now seventy-nine. He was born in Ohio of English-Dutch ancestry. His father was a farmer and grain dealer, not very successful.

When Edison was about eight years old he was sent to school. Three months later the teacher sent him home with a note saying that he was too stupid to teach.

Edison never had any more schooling. His mother, who was a clever and good woman, taught him herself.

He was always a queer boy. Once, when he was six, he was found sitting on goose eggs trying to hatch them.

On another occasion he made a grand experiment in a barn and burned it down, for which he got a good thrashing.

He was always fond of chemistry. He had a laboratory of 200 bottles in his home. He marked every one "Poison" so that nobody would touch them.

At fourteen he became a newsboy, selling magazines and papers on railway trains. He had a small laboratory on the train. Finally, he set fire to the train, and the guard threw him out, and his bottles after him. Also, he boxed the boy's ears so hard that he has been deaf ever since.

At sixteen he became a telegraph boy in Canada; but he lost his job because of a labor-saving invention — the boss said he was lazy. He lost three more jobs in the same way.

At twenty-three he wandered to New York. He arrived penniless. He got a job in a stock-ticker office. This was his first good fortune. He was paid well because he was able to repair a valuable machine which had broken down.

The following year he invented a telegraphic machine and sold it to the Western Union Telegraph Company for $40,000. He would have been glad to take $400 for it, as he had no idea of the value of his inventions at that time.

He used the $40,000 to start a machine shop. Then, in 1873, he visited England for the first time and sold some of his inventions.

One English firm sent him an offer of "thirty thousand" for one of his patents. Edison thought it meant 30,000 dollars — he said "Yes." To his amazement he received 30,000 POUNDS — five times as much.

Edison is the most prolific inventor in the world. He has taken out over 1,000 patents. He has been a professional inventor for half-a-century. He is the most persevering of all experimenters. He works harder and sleeps less than any other man. He cares nothing for money. He smokes and chews tobacco.

He hates new clothes. He has not been measured for a new suit for thirty years. He was measured then by a certain tailor, and he simply tells the tailor, "I want another suit off that jig pattern."

He has had many failures and a few wonderful successes. Once he spent two years and $2,000,000 on an invention which proved to be of little value.

He cares little for honors. An English University offered him an honor, and he has never bothered to go and get it. Once he was awarded a gold medal in New York. He lost it on a ferry-boat on the way home. "Never mind," he said to his wife, "I have a couple of quarts of them upstairs."

The last time he was in France he was given the Cross of the Legion of Honor. He accepted the Cross, but when it came to putting the sash on he backed up and would not allow it.

His inventions have done much to add to the comfort and happiness of the world. His whole life, in fact, has been spent in social service.

Edison never has an idle moment. Even in his play he is inventing. I have seen him on several occasions in his long, narrow laboratory in New Jersey, digging, digging, always digging into some difficult problem.

One peculiar thing about Edison is that he seldom believes anything until he proves it. He has a vast store of doubt with regard to the opinions and practices of men.

In his library there are more than 10,000 books, mostly on scientific subjects. But Edison seldom believes a single statement in any of these books until he puts it to the test and proves it.

In his work he takes a book only as a starting-point. It is only a place to begin. It is not final.

He has spent his whole life exploring the No Man's Land which exists outside of the books.

Edison is, first and foremost, a hard worker. He detests laziness as the worst of all diseases. He will employ a stupid man, but never a lazy one.

Edison takes nothing for granted. He dislikes the man who is flashy and superficial. In everything he does he digs down to the roots. He has spent his whole life FINDING OUT WHY.

MICHAEL FARADAY

LONDON wasn't much of a city in 1796. Neither was Bermondsey much of a place at that time in London. Neither was Jacob Street much of a place in Bermondsey. Neither was the livery stable much of a place in Jacob Street.

And above this livery stable there were a few rooms to let, and they were taken by a Yorkshire blacksmith who had four little kiddies.

And one of these kiddies was a quiet little chap, five years old, named Michael. The father's name was Faraday.

Not much of a start in life, was it? Yet that little Michael grew up to be the FOUNDER OF ELECTRICAL SCIENCE.

He became one of the most profound THINKERS of the world — in many respects the foremost SCIENTIST of his day.

More than this even, he was one of the simplest, gentlest, noblest and most lovable men who have ever ripened out of the human race.

Perhaps somewhere in a quiet corner of

Heaven there is a little group of congenial spirits talking about the laws of the universe, with Newton there, and Franklin, and Darwin, and Wallace, and Huxley and Pasteur, and in the center Faraday, with his shining face, telling them how to explain scientific facts to little children.

Young Michael Faraday was not born with a golden spoon in his mouth. Many a time, because of the high price of food, and the low wages of blacksmiths, he had no spoon at all. In fact, his mother gave him a loaf of bread once a week — that was all he had.

As for schooling, he had little or none. He had to earn pennies as soon as he could walk.

It is a fact worth noting that Faraday, who became one of the most cultured men in England, never saw Oxford until he went there to teach its professors.

At thirteen, young Michael was lucky. He was engaged as errand-boy in a bookseller's shop. Here, for the first time, he had NEWSPAPERS and BOOKS.

One glorious day, when he was fourteen, he found a little book on CHEMISTRY. At that moment his career began.

He began to make experiments in the evenings. He lived in a tiny bedroom in the bookseller's house; and there was a kindly cook who gave him materials out of her pantry for these experiments.

At twenty-one he received a present that was worth more to him than the gold of the Bank of England. One of his customers gave him a ticket for a course of lectures by Sir Humphry Davy, who was the greatest chemist of his day.

People noticed him at the lectures — a slim, pale lad with large keen eyes. He was the youngest person present. He took notes and made them into an illustrated book.

At this point he threw luck aside and decided to act for himself. He wrote to Sir Humphry Davy, sent his book of notes and asked for a job as an apprentice of science.

Sir Humphry sent for him, liked him, and got him a job as assistant in the laboratory of the Royal Institution. He started at $6 a week.

He had now found his own ladder to fame and up he went steadily to the top.

His first task was to accompany Sir Humphry himself on a two years' trip through Europe. In this way he met the scientists of Paris, Genoa, Florence, Rome, Naples and Geneva. At twenty-five, he published his first article on science. Then, at twenty-nine, he made his great discovery that a magnet will REVOLVE continuously around a magnetic current. This was the birth of the electric motor. Faraday made this discovery fully a century ago.

When thirty, he fell in love and married a simple girl who sat in the next pew in the little chapel where he worshiped every Sunday. Her name was Sarah Barnard.

They lived happily ever afterwards — for forty-six years — but had no children.

At thirty-two he was one of the world's leading scientists. He was a member of the Royal Society and a Director in the Royal Institution, where he began at $6 a week.

He now had a chance to be rich. Large sums of money were offered to him for his help as a chemist. But he and his wife talked the matter over and they decided that he had no time to be rich.

He started a twenty-three-year job, writing his great book on "Experimental Researches in Electricity." This book changed electrical science from dawn to day. It was written fully seventy-five years ago and in many respects it is not outgrown yet.

Faraday was a philosopher as well as a scientist. The great passion of his life was to show that the universe consists of ONE SINGLE ENERGY, not of seventy or eighty separate elements.

His mind reached out for the complete circle of truth. He climbed from facts to principles and from principles to sympathy. He felt that the whole world was kin — plants, elements, animals, people and all.

He was a MAN — so gentle that children gathered around him wherever he went; and so strong that he compelled an apology from Lord Melbourne — an ass who happened to be Prime Minister.

Faraday and his wife spent their last years in a cottage near Hampton Court. It was lent to him by Queen Victoria. Here he told the fairy tales of science to children who sat on his knee, and to the wisest scientists who came from all parts of the world to see the master.

HE HAD A HAPPY LIFE. HE DID WHAT HE WANTED TO DO. HE SUCCEEDED BEYOND HIS DREAMS. HE LIVED LONG AND HE LIVED NOBLY.

JOSEPH FELS

JOSEPH FELS was the smallest man I have ever known. He was no larger than a twelve-year-old boy. But in mind and heart he was one of the greatest and noblest men of his generation.

He was so lovable that it is hard to write about him without being carried away and saying too much. He was a man of friends. He made friends easily and he held them.

He had a wonderful life. He rose from poverty to great wealth without robbing anybody; and he lavished his money to help people and to remedy the injustices of the world. He died in 1914, just before the War began.

If ever a man was moved to the depths by human misery in any form, that man was Joseph Fels. He was more like a mother than a man. He was a millionaire, yet he marched to Hyde Park with the unemployed in 1905.

Joseph Fels was born in a tiny cottage in Virginia. His father was a hard-working man, but not very successful. He was a maker of toilet soap.

Joseph did badly at school, as the best boys usually do. He disliked the routine and the memorizing. At fifteen he rebelled and refused to go to school any longer.

He became a soap salesman. He saved his money and at twenty-two he bought a little soap factory for $4,000 and became a manufacturer.

For fifteen years he gave all his energies to his business. He took his brothers in with him as partners.

As competition was keen in the soap business, he saw the necessity for a specialty. He found one — a naphtha soap that would clean clothes more easily. He bought the rights to this soap and it made his fortune. It is now used all over the world.

At twenty he fell in love with a girl of great ability and charm. She, too, was small in stature. They were perfectly mated and very happy. The only trouble, so far as I know, that ever entered their home was when the baby died. Fels had a passion for children, and never quite recovered from this loss.

As soon as he became rich, he gave most of his time to social problems. He stopped working for himself and began to work for others.

Two things Joseph Fels hated, as far as his nature would allow him to hate anything; and these two things were WASTE and INJUSTICE.

You see, he was half a business man and half an apostle. He believed in success and goodness, both.

He did not believe that money alone could do any good; and neither did he believe in preaching heaven-on-earth to people who were being treated unjustly.

The greatest waste in England, he said, was the IDLE LAND. There it lay, 30,000,000 acres, while 50,000 idle workers clamored for bread.

IDLE LAND AND IDLE MEN! Why in the name of humanity and common sense cannot these two be got together, so as to abolish the idleness of both? This was the question that Joseph Fels put to the statesmen of England, and not one of them has answered it yet.

There is still the idle land and there are still the idle men — ex-soldiers and ex-sailors — tens of thousands of them.

To Fels, the crime of crimes was to establish a palace for one man in the midst of 10,000 idle acres, while 200 families were huddled together in squalid slums, without a foot of earth to call their own.

Fels disliked poverty and luxury, both. He regarded both as being injurious to people. No man should be left with nothing, he thought, and no man should have too much.

He put PEOPLE ahead of everything, ahead of finance and business and heredity and aristocracy and government. Truly, he was a remarkable millionaire.

Once when talking to a Chamber of Commerce, he said, "I own in a certain city eleven and a half acres of land, for which I paid $32,500 a few years ago. On account of the increase of population in that city my land is now worth $125,000. I have done nothing to cause that increase in value. My fellow-citizens created it, and I believe that it belongs to them and not to me. I believe that we should take these community-values for our common purposes instead of taxing enterprise and industry."

Fels spent thousands in spreading his ideas on the-land-for-the-people. He once sent a packet of leaflets to every voter in Great Britain. He attended every Trade Union Congress for years.

Many stories are told of his originality and kindness of heart. Here are a few of them:

Once he had promised to buy a donkey for a little five-year-old girl. Soon afterwards he arrived at the house, leading a donkey, and followed by a little new-born donkey. He was asked, "Why did you buy two?" He replied, "You see, I couldn't separate mother and baby, so I bought them both."

At a dinner party he sat beside a lady who sought to impress upon him her superior quality. In describing a certain man, she said, "Of course, he is not of our kind." Fels asked quietly, "Isn't everyone of our kind?"

When he built a house at Bickley, in Kent, he had these lines engraved on the front door —
>What I spent I had!
>What I saved I lost!
>What I gave I have!

On one occasion, when he spoke at Balliol College, Oxford, he began his lecture by saying, "I'm going to talk to you about the land, this earth you're living on. Who made it? Who does it belong to? Who has a right to it? And how can learning flourish in a nation that permits injustice?"

On another occasion, he startled a London audience by saying, "Within a bus ride of the Bank of England there are 10,000 acres lying idle. This land, properly cultivated, would support 8,000 families."

Joseph Fels was a human shuttle. He wove together all manner of people.

He was a landlord, yet he asked to have his land taxed more heavily. He was a capitalist, yet he supported the candidates of the Labor Party.

He was a man of the TRUTH. He fought against Stupidity and Cruelty all his life. He made the world gentler and more intelligent.

One of his closest friends was George Lansbury, editor and Labor Leader, and Fels was a Capitalist, yet they were devoted companions. Lansbury once wrote of Fels as follows:

"I met Joseph Fels in the summer of 1903. He came to my house like a breath of fresh air. His transparent honesty of purpose, his love of humanity, were clear to us all.

"I had heard very little of him, and I confess I was somewhat prejudiced against him because he was a rich American. But five minutes' talk with him dispelled my doubts and fears, and we then commenced a close and intimate friendship that will never really end.

"He made me realize as never before that it is worth while to struggle and fight for great causes and inspired me with faith in my fellowmen."

There! That is a Labor Leader talking of a Capitalist. Does it not show that all class distinction and wealth distinction are very small matters indeed, and that all right-hearted men are co-workers and friends?

HENRY FORD

JUDGING by results, Henry Ford is the most successful manufacturer in the world.

He pays the highest wages.

He makes the highest profits.

He sells the cheapest goods.

Henry Ford is a complete answer to the silly Marxian theory that a capitalist can only make money by robbing his employees or the public.

Henry Ford robs nobody. He is not an exploiter of the proletariat.

He is a multi-millionaire, and every penny of his money is clean.

His enormous profits are only a part of what he saves the public; and he pays his workers far more than they could make if they were on their own.

Henry Ford is a capitalist, and he shows all capitalists a better way of getting rich.

He made his own success — he and his men together. He has no title. He would never accept one. He is not even a "Mr." His friends call him Henry.

He was born on a small farm near Detroit in 1863. His father was an Irish emigrant.

At school Henry Ford was a sort of dunce. The teacher could do little with him.

Henry was fed up with school by the time he was fifteen, so he ran away and got a job in an engine-works. He started at $2.50 a week.

Several years later he returned to the farm, but the best thing he did while on the farm was to marry a neighbor's daughter.

One evening, as he was reading a farm paper, he saw a picture of a new horseless carriage invented by a Frenchman.

He was fascinated. That picture gripped him and changed the whole course of his life.

He neglected his farm and began to build a horseless carriage in his barn. He put an old engine on an old buggy and forthwith became the joke of the county.

There are several old men and women in the poorhouses of America who once had a grand time, laughing at Henry Ford.

Presently, against the advice of everybody, he left the farm and went to Detroit. He got a mechanic's job at $150 a month, and at nights he worked on his horseless carriage.

He made one that had one cylinder — a

rickety, wheezy, ridiculous thing. BUT IT MOVED.

He improved this absurd motor for eight long years. At last he built a good motor — so good that he won a race with it.

At one bound he and his motor became famous. He won other races. He even beat Barney Oldfield, who was the best known racer of those days.

Several friends lent him $15,000, and he started a small motor works. He secured the ablest managers. He paid them well and they organized his immense business.

He is a slim, athletic, sun-tanned man. He has not been spoiled by power and wealth. The last time I saw him, at his Detroit Works, he was showing his telephone girl how to operate her switchboard.

He is not a business man in the usual sense. He is a mechanic — an inventor. HE MADE HIS SUCCESS BY APPRECIATING THE PRINCIPLE OF STANDARDIZATION.

We may scoff at him if we like — if we are foolish enough; but it seems to me that he is the one who has the joke on the rest of us.

HENRY FORD KNOWS HOW. He has solved his business problems. He has shown us the one right way to handle men and produce goods and make profits without making enemies.

It would be better for all of us if we STUDIED Ford more and scoffed at him less. The more I find out about him the more I am impressed with his ability and his sense.

What the world needs is more Henry Fords; that is the truth, whether we like it or not.

If we had 1,000 Fords, we would have high wages, high profits, low prices and no labor troubles. We would have peace and prosperity.

Take, for instance, Ford's methods as an EMPLOYER. In this respect he is most peculiar. He has followed a most unusual course, and he has made a great success of it.

The fact is, that Henry Ford seems to regard himself as a LABOR LEADER rather than an employer.

He gives his men MORE than they ask.

He gives them better working conditions than they had ever thought of.

He watches over them and protects them. He has made his men the best-paid and most contented workers the world has ever seen.

No labor leader has done as much for labor as Henry Ford has.

He has never called them out on strike. He has never made them pay dues. He has led them to success, not to failure.

In 1914 his workers were contented, but he suddenly DOUBLED their wages. As a result, in 1915 he made more net profit than he had ever made before.

He protects his workers from any injustice. He has 2,000 foremen, and not one of them can discharge a worker.

In 1919, out of over 50,000 workers, ONLY 118 were discharged.

There is a special staff of thirty men, who investigate all troubles between the foremen and the workers. A foreman who has frequent troubles with his men will soon be called into the manager's office and told of the error of his ways.

Ford has nothing against unionism, but he outdoes it at every point. He regards unionism as a necessary protection against stupid or oppressive employers, but he is neither stupid nor oppressive.

There is nothing merciless nor ruthless in his factory. In fact, it is a most gentle and humane institution. It is more sympathetic and tenderhearted than most churches.

For instance, there are 400 workers in Ford's who are ex-convicts. They were cast out as felons, but Ford has given them a chance. He has restored them to self-respect, and they are leading honest and happy lives.

There are 2,000 weak or crippled men in the Ford factory. They wear a button that says, "For light work only."

One of Ford's obstinate theories is that he must take his share of the crippled, the criminal and the blind. One of his most competent workers is a blind man.

He spares no expense to give his men the best conditions in the works. He has a special staff of 700 painters, window-washers, carpenters, etc., to keep everything clean and bright. The shop floor is as clean as the floor of a kitchen.

The air is changed every twelve minutes. All the smoke and gas in the foundry is carried off. There are no cold nor over-heated rooms.

As to "speeding up," John R. Commons lately visited the Ford factory; and he reports that he saw no speeding up, "except in some parts of the foundry, among the new workers."

He has moved his whole business high above strikes and lockouts.

He has stopped the war between the workers and the management. He has established peace and goodwill.

HE HAS SHOWN EVERY OTHER EMPLOYER WHAT CAN BE DONE.

KING C. GILLETTE

"WHO is the most remarkable salesman you have ever known?" asked a friend.

This was not an easy question, but after a moment's thought I replied — "GILLETTE, the inventor of the safety razor."

In my opinion, he was the most remarkable because he was a salesman, an inventor, an idealist, a manufacturer and a financier.

He made money happily, no doubt about that. He made a success in five entirely different lines — who else has done that?

Few people know the extraordinary story of Gillette. He lived in London during 1904, when he was selling "Crown Seal" corks in London, but at that time his razor was a failure and quite unknown.

His photograph is in every town in the world, almost in every street, as it is on the cover of every razor blade.

In the last seventeen years he has built up a company that is worth $30,000,000; with net profits of $7,500,000 a year.

He has three factories — in England, Canada

and the United States. He created an entirely new type of razor and he has sold it to millions of men at a good price.

He is still alive and full of new ideas. His latest hobby is the NERACAR — a new kind of motor cycle.

He is seventy-one years old and a citizen of the world. He has lived in London, Paris, Florida and New York. At present he is in California.

Gillette's full name is King Camp Gillette. He was born in a small town in the forests of Wisconsin. His father was a struggling business man, sometimes up and sometimes down.

When young Gillette was seventeen, his father lost everything by a fire, and the lad had to make his own living.

At twenty-one he was a salesman. He was a visionary man, fond of new ideas.

I knew him in 1894. He came to a series of lectures I was giving, and afterwards he sent me a copy of a book he had written.

He had written this book about a new type of house that he had invented — a huge structure in the shape of a dome, large enough to contain several hundred families.

He and I, both, in those days were trying to

find a way to abolish slums. We believed that poverty was preventable and we maintained that the supreme crime of the world was to allow children to be born in the midst of filth and squalor.

Gillette's father was an inventor, of a sort; and in his spare moments, Gillette was always inventing things. He always had the idea that some day he would invent something wonderful and make his fortune by it.

At thirty-six, he met a rich inventor — William Painter, who had originated the "Crown Seal" metal cork, which is now used on beer and mineral water bottles.

One day, Painter said to Gillette — "Why don't you invent something that makes a man keep on buying from you as long as he lives? No use selling just one thing to a man. Sell him something that he uses and throws away."

This suggestion was the originating cause of the Gillette razor. Gillette thought about it for weeks — how to invent a PERISHABLE NECESSITY.

Then, one morning, he was shaving himself. The razor was dull. His beard was stiff. He was scraping away painfully at his face, when, in a flash, he thought — why not invent a better kind of razor?

WHY NOT INVENT ONE WITH A REMOVABLE EDGE?

He put down his razor and with the lather on his face, began to sketch out the design of a new razor, which would consist of a blade and a blade-container.

In half an hour he had made his plan. Then he finished scraping his face and rushed out to an ironmonger's to buy some steel tape and a file.

He made his first razor himself and had it patented. That was in 1895. He was forty years old before his great success began.

At first, his razor was a failure. It was a joke for nine years. His friends, and he always had plenty of them, chaffed him unmercifully about his freak razor.

Gillette and his silly razor were laughed at for nine years — that is the point to remember. Every capitalist who met Gillette during those nine years might have had some of the Gillette shares for a song.

In 1901, Gillette found a master mechanic — W. E. Nickerson. He was a man of unusual skill. He perfected the razor and a company was formed.

But up to 1902, not one razor was sold. In desperation, Gillette began giving them away.

He gave one to a business man named John Joyce. Joyce shaved with it. He liked it. He agreed to buy $60,000 worth of shares.

The little razor company then began to sell a few razors, but Gillette had to support himself and his family by selling steel corks.

In 1904, the right advertising man came on the scene. He was the last link in the chain of success.

The razors began to sell. Money fell on Gillette in thousands. His old employer, in the steel cork business, bought $40,000 of shares and has been glad of it ever since.

Gillette was wise enough to keep a large number of shares for himself. So, at forty-nine years of age, Gillette had made his dream come true.

He had invented a PERISHABLE NECESSITY. He had invented something which compelled buyers to become permanent customers.

From first to last, please notice, Gillette's success was a matter of IDEAS. He first got an idea and then he put his will behind it.

He was a failure at forty-nine, you might say; but he has had money and fame ever since.

King C. Gillette always put IDEAS FIRST, and he always had large ideas. He created a new

IDEA. He shaped this IDEA into a FACT; and then he sold this FACT to the clean-shaven men of the civilized world.

That is why I would call him the greatest SALESMAN I have ever known.

WARREN HASTINGS

HERE is a story of one of the greatest Englishmen who ever lived, a lad who became the ruler of 50,000,000 people.

A penniless orphan who made himself the despot of India!

A poorly paid young clerk who rose to be the ablest warrior and statesman of his day!

The one man who established British rule in India, in spite of enemies abroad and fools at home!

Such was Warren Hastings.

He was born in a little English village in 1732. At the age of twelve he was an orphan — without either parents or property.

As he grew up, he was an under-sized, half-fed lad. If ever a boy was chucked into the deep waters of life, to sink or swim, he was.

At eight, an uncle appeared and sent young Warren to a school in London. Here he was noted as a good boatman, swimmer and scholar. At fourteen he was top boy in the school.

All was going well with him until his good uncle died. Then he had to shift for himself.

So, at seventeen, he went to India as a clerk of the East India Company.

After several years of clerking he was suddenly caught in the midst of an Indian rebellion. He was flung into jail and nearly into the Black Hole of Calcutta.

He escaped and joined Robert Clive, who had just begun his great career. Hastings was seven years younger than Clive. The two became firm friends.

At thirty-two he returned to England. He was now moderately rich, but he soon spent his money on books and friends. He associated with men of letters. Cowper, the poet, was his lifelong friend.

In four years, for lack of money, he was forced to return to India. On the ship he fell ill, and was nursed back to health by a beautiful Russian girl, who had married a rascally German Baron.

He fell in love with her, enabled her to secure a divorce, married, and remained a devoted husband for life. This affair caused endless scandal, although now that he is dead every one admits that he was as pure and honorable a man as ever lived.

He promised to make his wife the Queen of

India, and he did. He soon became an uncrowned king. He put Nabobs up and pulled them down. He had only a handful of redcoats, but he held the territory that Clive had captured, and added to it.

If Warren Hastings had been left alone he would have solved the problems of Indian Government, and prevented the troubles of to-day, but he was not left alone.

The directors of the East India Company constantly clamored for more money. They compelled Hastings to take the treasure of the Nabobs and to send it to London.

Hastings robbed India, or rather he robbed the robbers of India. But that was nothing new. India had always been robbed — most of all by her native rulers.

There was never so little robbing as there was under Hastings. He did his best to put down all robbery and oppression, and he gave India the best government it ever had.

Then the politicians of Westminster began to interfere in matters of which they had no knowledge. They passed the "Regulating Act," to take away the power of Hastings.

This, of course, encouraged the Indian revolutionists, and Hastings soon had a war on his hands. He seized the leader of the rebels — a Brahmin called Nuncomar — tried him and hanged him in broad daylight before thousands of natives.

It was a terrible cure for a terrible danger. After that there were no rebellions, and not an Indian dared lift a finger or wag a tongue at Hastings.

Both Parliament and the East India Company attacked him. He was ordered to resign. HE REFUSED. He was 15,000 miles from London and he was determined that Britain should not lose India.

Next the Supreme Court of India tried to take control; but Hastings at once opposed his soldiers to the sheriffs and put the judges in their place.

Then came a war with Hyder Ali — the ablest of the Indian generals. Parliament at once backed down and begged Hastings to do as he liked.

Hastings trained his little army and attacked Hyder Ali in the great battle of Porto Novo. Hyder Ali was defeated. If Hastings had resigned, India would probably have been lost.

Just to make his victory complete, Hastings actually took fifty redcoats and captured the rich city of Benares. He seized the Rajah, held the palace against an army, and won by sheer audacity.

Then he settled down to create a fair, just system of government for India. He was trusted by the natives. He spoke several of their languages and he was sincerely fond of them.

HE ESTABLISHED PEACE IN INDIA. And with one exception there has been peace ever since.

Hastings held India at a time when the British Empire was falling to pieces. It was during the reign of the crazy German King — George III.

America had been lost. So had Senegal, Goree and Minorca. India, too, would have gone if Hastings had not held it single-handed.

If he had been a man of a different nationality he would probably have made himself the emperor of India and founded a dynasty.

At fifty-three his job was finished and well done; so he returned home to spend the rest of his days in his beloved Worcester.

To his amazement he was attacked on all sides for being cruel and corrupt — he who had done more to stop cruelty and corruption than any man of his generation.

Parliament voted to impeach him — 119 to

79. Burke, who was now old and irascible, led the attack. Hastings was arrested. He was tried in a shameful trial that lasted for eight years.

This trial was a national disgrace. At last, he was found not guilty — twenty-three votes to six.

By this time nearly all his money had been spent, so he and his wife went to the village of Daylesford where he was born.

Here he bought a farm and lived quietly for twenty-three years, among his cattle, his books and his friends. He was never embittered by his country's ingratitude. He took it all as part of the interesting game of life, in which he had been for a time a champion player.

Shortly before he died, he was sent for by Parliament and given a grand ovation. Honors were showered upon him.

So, after all, he died with a smile; and out in Benares the natives erected a temple to his memory.

WARREN HASTINGS KEPT INDIA BRITISH, AND IT HAS REMAINED SO FOR 150 YEARS.

ELIAS HOWE

FROM this story of Elias Howe, the inventor of the sewing machine, you will see what REAL troubles are.

Elias Howe benefited nearly the whole human race.

He won fame and fortune in the end but his life was a desperate struggle against poverty, stupidity, illness and death.

Nothing — not even starvation — could make him give up his life-work. The story of his life is an inspiration to us all. It shows what one determined man, plus a new idea, can do to benefit the world.

Elias Howe was born in the United States in 1819. At that time there was no sewing machine. There was not even an idea of it. No woman thought of such a thing.

Little Elias was not pampered as a child. He was one of a family of eight. His father was a poor flour-miller, with ten mouths to feed.

Elias was a frail little chap. His body was far too weak for his mind. He was lame, too, as well as delicate.

At six years of age he had to go to work. He limped every weekday to his father's mill and helped his brothers and sisters to stick wire teeth through leather straps. It was this task, very likely, that made him think of a sewing machine.

At sixteen he set out for the city of Lowell, Mass., as he had heard a man tell of its wonderful mills and great machines.

He worked in a cotton mill for two years, and then found a place in a machine-shop. This job suited him well, as he was a natural mechanic.

At twenty-one he married. Soon he had three children — more family than wages. They lived in a shabby little house and had to make every penny do the work of two.

His work was hard — so hard that he was often too tired at night to eat his supper. As he told his wife once, he often wished he could "lie in bed for ever and ever."

When he was twenty-five years old a fellow worker said to him one day — "What a great thing it would be if some one could invent a machine for SEWING!"

This chance remark woke up Howe's brain. He was really one of the ablest inventors in the world, but he was not aware of it. He did not know his own powers.

First, he watched his wife sew. Then he made a machine which operated a needle that pointed at both ends, with the eye in the middle. He was trying to make a machine that would imitate his wife's hand. This was a failure.

Suddenly a new idea flashed into his brain — why imitate hand-sewing? Why not invent a new way of sewing, which would make a sewing machine possible?

Immediately he thought of the plan of using TWO threads instead of one. He invented the shuttle and a curved needle with an eye NEAR THE POINT.

In a flash he had solved the problem. No one had ever thought of such a thing. He had invented a practical sewing machine.

In great joy he gave up his job and moved with his family to his father's house to complete his great invention. He set up a little workshop in the garret and began to save money to buy a second-hand lathe.

Then came a fire and everything was swept away. Howe saved his precious model, but little else.

At this crisis a coal and wood dealer stepped in and said — "I'll let you board in my house and give you $500 for one half of your patent."

Howe agreed. He fitted up another workshop and in six months he made a machine that sewed the seams of two woollen suits — one for the coal and wood merchant and one for himself.

His task was done. So he thought. He did not know that every new idea has to fight its way in the world against the very people whom it will benefit most.

After invention comes SALESMANSHIP, but Howe didn't know that.

He ran triumphantly with his sewing machine to the tailors of Boston. They admired it as a "cute contrivance." But they said: "We don't want it. It would ruin our trade."

He took it from firm to firm, but not one man would invest a penny in it. This discouraged the coal and wood merchant, and he withdrew from the partnership and asked Howe to move elsewhere.

Howe had neither money nor friends. To support his family he became an engine-driver on a railway.

Then he fell ill. So did his wife. If it had not been for several kindly neighbors the whole Howe family might have been wiped out, sewing-machine and all.

When he recovered his health he scraped together enough money to buy a steerage ticket to London. He believed that England would treat him better than America had done.

Here, again, he was mistaken. He found no one to help him. One man on Cheapside bought his first machine for $1,250, and gave Howe a job at $15 a week.

Howe worked for this man for eight months, but found him too hard an employer and left him. He had no money, and often there were days when he and his family sat starving in the great city of London.

He had offered England his sewing machine, and England had refused it.

Starvation compelled him to go back to America. He pawned his model for enough money to send his wife and children back. A few months later he went back himself as his wife wrote that she was dying of consumption.

He arrived in New York with sixty cents in his pocket. He still had 250 miles to go. He went into a machine-shop and worked for several days to earn money to pay his railway fare.

When he arrived home his wife was dead.

Weakened and heartbroken, he still persevered. He made a new model. A business man named Bliss lent him some money. He built more machines and eventually sold them.

The demand for machines increased, and in twelve years Howe was a millionaire.

He received the gold medal of the Paris Exposition in 1867 and the Cross of the Legion of Honor.

He could endure the hardships and the hunger and the losses, but it seemed that he could not stand the fame and fortune. A few weeks after he received the Cross of the Legion of Honor he died.

He had finished his course. He had fought the good fight. He had succeeded.

THOMAS HENRY HUXLEY

THE story of Thomas Henry Huxley ought to be told to every generation.

Huxley was a FIGHTING SCIENTIST. He battled in the cause of science. He struck down superstition and ignorance. He fought for clear thinking — for Efficiency and commonsense.

Huxley was for thirty years the voice of science crying in the wilderness of tradition and custom. He was a prophet. He was the wisest teacher of his day.

Huxley was born at Ealing, England, in 1825. Ealing was then a country village, and Huxley's father was a teacher in the village school.

There was very little money in the Huxley home, but there were BOOKS. Also, there were wonderful conversations on great subjects. These two — the books and the talks — gave young Huxley his real education. From school, he said, he learned little.

As a boy he had an active, inquiring mind. He was always asking — "Why?" At fifteen he tried to solve the problem of the colors of the sunset. At seventeen he tried to classify all knowledge under two heads — Mind and Nature.

His two sisters both married doctors, so at fifteen he was taken from school and sent to study medicine. He paid little attention to the lectures on medicine, but he was fascinated with a certain big MICROSCOPE.

This microscope showed him the marvels of Nature. It opened up a world of tiny things to which our eyes are blind. He ran to his precious microscope every night; and at nineteen he made his first discovery — he found a membrane in the root of the human hair. This membrane is now known as "Huxley's layer."

He invented what he fondly believed a perpetual motion machine at nineteen, and was so excited about it that he took it to Faraday. Faraday gave him a kindly hearing, but told him that perpetual motion was impossible. "If it were possible," said Faraday, "it would have occurred spontaneously in Nature, and would have overpowered all the other forces."

At twenty he secured his medical degree. Then a friend pushed him into the navy, and by an extraordinary bit of luck he was made assistant surgeon on a war vessel which was going for a scientific cruise in the Tropics. Like Darwin and Hooker, Huxley got his start as a scientist on board a British man-of-war.

At Sydney he met a young English girl — Netty Heathorn. It was love at first sight. She later became his wife. They were pals and inseparable companions for forty years.

Huxley had four years on board ship, and these four years made him a scientist. He gathered a great deal of valuable information on plants and fishes. The Admiralty allowed him $1,500 to publish his facts, and he at once became known as a naturalist.

At twenty-five he married. He was earning $1,000 a year as a professor in a London college, and $1,000 more by writing for magazines.

At this time he began lecturing to working men. He always believed that in the end labor would be the best friend of science.

"I want the working classes to understand that science has great facts for them. I am sick of the dilettante middle class, and I mean to try what I can do with these hard-handed fellows who live among FACTS."

At thirty-one he wrote out a CREED for himself. Here it is:

"To smite all humbugs, however big;

"To give a nobler tone to science;

"To set an example of abstinence from petty personal controversies and of toleration for everything but lying;

"To be indifferent as to whether the work is recognized as mine or not, so long as it is done."

Huxley was tortured by aches and pains all his life, but he refused to be ill. He worked from 9 a.m. until midnight — most of the time on jobs that brought him no payment at all.

In 1859 Darwin's great book, "Origin of Species," was printed. It proved the theory of Evolution, which is now believed by all civilized people.

It was a new doctrine then, and there was a roar of opposition against it. Darwin was not a fighter. He was a quiet, gentle thinker. It looked as though Evolution would be roared down; and perhaps it would have been if it had not been for Huxley.

He sprang to the front. He struck back. He gave blow for blow, and he was so able that the old fogeys learned to fear him.

Huxley was a man of the truth. "My business," he said, "is to teach my aspirations to conform themselves to facts, not to try and make facts harmonize with my aspirations."

He helped every good cause. He did not merely BELIEVE in certain reforms. He FOUGHT for them. He fought for freedom of the negro and for the emancipation of women. He fought for a more practical system of education.

In spite of ill-health and bereavement and poverty, he attacked the absurdities and the superstitions then dominant. He did not destroy them, but he beat them back off the main highway of progress.

Many a time he was at his wits' end for money. Once he had to sell his gold medal for $250. A wealthy friend offered him a pension of $2,000 a year but he refused it, preferring his independence to all else.

In 1876 he visited the United States, and startled the Americans by his clear, straight thinking. He addressed a great audience at Baltimore, and as they sat waiting to be flattered, he said:

"I cannot say that I am in the slightest degree impressed by your bigness and your material resources. Size is not grandeur. Territory does not make a nation. The great question is: What are you going to do with all these things? The one condition of success is the moral worth and intellectual clearness of the individual citizen."

As early as 1887 — long before Taylor and Emerson — Huxley advocated scientific management. He said, "We must have a scientific organization of our industries. It is indispensable to our prosperity."

He was a man of striking appearance — square forehead, square jaw, firm mouth, and deep-set flashing eyes. He suggested strength and straightforwardness. He was a master of clear, forcible language. Those who heard him will never forget his magnetism and sincerity.

Huxley was a pioneer. He was ahead of his generation. He was ahead of us who are alive to-day.

HE TAUGHT US THAT, IN THE LONG RUN, THERE IS NOTHING SO PRACTICAL OR SO PROFITABLE OR SO MORAL AS THE TRUTH.

GEORGE F. JOHNSON

I OUGHT to begin this article — "Once upon a time," but the truth is that I shall be describing the largest and most profitable shoe factory in the world. So it is not a fairy tale. It is a story of EFFICIENCY, in the widest human sense.

There is a beautiful valley in the United States, about 100 miles from New York. The people who live there call it "THE VALLEY OF FAIR PLAY."

There are two towns, side by side, in this valley, called JOHNSON and ENDICOTT.

About 50,000 people live in the valley, and 15,000 of them work in two large shoe factories, belonging to the Endicott-Johnson Company.

THEY MAKE 81,000 PAIRS OF SHOES A DAY.

THE VALUE OF THEIR OUTPUT IN ONE YEAR WAS MORE THAN $140,000,000.

You will see from these amazing figures that the people in this valley know how to WORK. There is no "ca'canny" in "The Valley of Fair Play."

But, if it were not for these figures, you would

think that the people in this valley cared about nothing but FUN.

There are no slums in the valley. There are no company houses. Most families own their own homes. The houses are built of wood and painted in bright colors.

Between the two towns there is a large tract of land called IDEAL PARK. Here there is a great swimming pool, free to everybody. Nearby there is a small pool for the kiddies. There is a roundabout, too, also free.

There is a DANCING PAVILION, open three evenings a week. Admission to dancers twenty-five cents.

There is the BALL GROUND, large enough for two games at the same time; and as the factories close down at 4.30, there are a couple of games every afternoon.

There is the RACE TRACK — a half-mile track, with stables and grand-stand. Every Saturday afternoon there are races, and at times there are as many as 100,000 people around the track.

There is the CLUB HOUSE, in the center of a grassy lawn, all embroidered with flower beds. This is the social center, where everybody meets everybody. It contains a free library and special rooms for boy scouts, and card-rooms and dining-rooms. It is a scene of jollity, every evening.

FUN! SOCIABILITY! EDUCATION! SPORT! MUSIC! These seem to be the main things in "The Valley of Fair Play"; and yet these jolly shoemakers make 81,000 pairs of shoes a day.

Their daily average output is ELEVEN SHOES APIECE, leather and all.

They believe, in this valley, that PLAY is the sunshine of life, and that everybody needs it as much as he needs food.

They believe in LAUGHTER and LOVE and HAPPINESS as much as they believe in MACHINERY and COAL-POWER and ORGANIZATION.

As you may have guessed, there is one man in this valley who is the founder of its success. His name is George F. Johnson, but everybody calls him "George F."

He lives in a handsome house near the park. He is always in sight. He lives, moves, and has his being in the midst of his people.

Any worker can see him in his office. If he is not in his office, he can be seen at the race track or in the dancing pavilion or at a ball game.

Usually he is in the middle of a crowd of children or a crowd of workers. The people are all the while consulting him on all sorts of matters. As they say — "He is the DADDY of our family."

Every kiddie on the street calls him "George F." Think of that and shudder, you frozen, stony-faced directors. Here is a man who does a business of $140,000,000 a year, who has time to fly kites and mend dolls.

One May Day the workers of this valley had a great parade of 20,000 workers, and whom do you suppose led it? GEORGE F. He walked at the head of his people, as every one expected him to do.

"You know, I LOVE all these people," he said to a friend as they sat in the grand-stand and waited for the next horse-race. "And I hope," he added, "that some of them love me."

He is not a philanthropist, this George F. Neither is he a genius nor a superman of any kind. He is just a big, sensible, good-hearted man, who likes to be in the middle of busy, happy people.

There is no suspicion and no snobbery in this valley. There is no "class consciousness," because there are no classes. Any worker has a chance to be a shareholder, and every capitalist works.

GEORGE F. JOHNSON

The entire body of 15,000 people, from George F. down to the door-boy at the tannery, all belong to the "E.-J. WORKERS."

Everything is done in the open. Any one can express an opinion. All the workers seem to feel that the whole place belongs to them.

FAIR PLAY AND FUN — there you have the secret of it all. That is the sort of EFFICIENCY that a wise person believes in — THE EFFICIENCY THAT PUTS PEOPLE FIRST AND THAT APPEALS TO THE HEARTS OF MEN AS WELL AS TO THE HEADS AND POCKETS.

George F. Johnson is now nearing eighty. He is the most successful of all shoe manufacturers; but forty years ago or so he was only a foreman of a small shoe factory that had gone to smash. His salary was less than $20 a week.

The chief creditor of this bankrupt little factory was a financier named Endicott. He went to see what could be done. He met George F. Johnson, and Johnson's sense and sincerity made a deep impression on him.

"I have no money," said Johnson, "but I can make a success of this factory. I don't care about salary, but you can sell me a half interest for $150,000 and I'll give you my note."

This was an amazing suggestion. It was absurd and risky, but Endicott was a wise man and he agreed. He bet $150,000 on Johnson.

The little factory succeeded with a bound. It grew until Johnson found himself "the Daddy of a 15,000 family."

The workers of his factory now live in two towns of their own called Endicott and Johnson.

They are not employees in the ordinary sense. They are PARTNERS. Just as Endicott made Johnson a partner, without asking him to pay for his shares, so Johnson has made partners of his workers.

Four-fifths of the employees are on piece-work and all of them share in the profits as soon as they have been one year in the factory.

Each year seven per cent. is paid on the preferred shares and ten per cent. on the ordinary shares. Then all the profit that is left is divided equally among the employees and the owners of the ordinary stock.

The company decides each year whether it will pay in cash or in ordinary shares. Usually the profit bonus amounts to fifty per cent. of a worker's wages.

The main difference between this Endicott-Johnson Company and other good firms seems to be that the workers do their full share. They give as well as get.

For instance, recently George F. Johnson presented the two towns with a magnificent statue by Moretti to commemorate the 1,692 employees who fought in the Great War.

The employees then in their turn presented Mr. Johnson with a handsome marble arch which they called "THE GATEWAY TO THE SQUARE DEAL TOWNS." The entire cost of the arch was borne by the workers.

On the one side of this arch is a bronze bust of George F. Johnson, and on the other is a bronze tablet inscribed with the Golden Rule — "As ye would that men should do unto you, do ye even so unto them."

George F., the Daddy of these two towns, frequently makes speeches to his people — straight, simple speeches, that are very effective. Here are a few of his sayings:

"I would rather have the confidence of you people than anything else in the world."

"In this company, if you do better you get the benefit yourselves. Nobody stands by to take it away from you."

"What we each want in this world is some one to make us do our best."

"You shouldn't leave it to me to drive the drones out of the hive, you should do it yourselves."

"We can lower our costs without lowering our wages if we will co-operate to lop off the non-producers — the barnacles and leeches."

"I am not asking you to do anything for ME. I am only asking you to do your best for yourselves; and the best you can do to-day is not the best you can do to-morrow."

"In this democratic business we must all ask ourselves — how many workers have we hired that we could get along without? How many are only a drag and an expense to us?"

"Don't be a burden! Don't create a handicap. Take your oar and pull. Don't backwater. Be worth while. Do your best. Give the old business a chance."

ISAAC NEWTON

SIR ISAAC NEWTON was the first of the whole human race, who found out the secret of the stars. He was the first to make known the mystery of Gravitation.

While you and I think about little matters — the rent, the wages, the profits, the output, and so forth — Isaac Newton thought of the UNIVERSE. His greatest book — "The Principia" — is generally acknowledged to be the greatest production of the human intellect.

Most great men seem to be born in accidental places, and Newton was no exception. He was born in a tiny hamlet in Lincolnshire in 1642. His father had died a few months after marriage, so the baby Newton came into the world fatherless. His mother had a little income of $400 a year.

As a boy Isaac Newton was a poor student. He was not interested in what the teacher said. He gave his whole attention to mechanical contrivances. He invented a windmill, a water-clock and a new sort of carriage which could be driven by the person who sat in it.

He was very fond of flying paper kites. He also made paper lanterns, and attached these lanterns to the tails of his kites. Then he flew the kites at night, so that the country people would believe that they were comets in the sky.

Even as a boy of twelve he was interested in mechanics and the heavens. He invented a sundial. He studied the stars. The mechanism of the heavens seemed to fascinate him.

When he was fifteen, he was put to work on a farm, but as a farm-boy he was entirely worthless. He would take a book on Astronomy and read it in a corner of a hedge, while the sheep were wandering and the cattle were eating the corn.

Fortunately, his mother appreciated his genius. She released him from farm work and sent him back to school.

When he was eighteen he was admitted into Trinity College, Cambridge. Nine years later he became a professor of Mathematics at Cambridge. His whole life practically was spent in connection with Cambridge.

When he was twenty-four he began to study the phenomena of light. He discovered that light was composed of several different sorts of rays. The red rays were different from the orange rays. The orange rays were different from the yellow rays, and so forth.

Next, he invented a reflecting telescope. It was the first of its kind. His first telescope is now in the library of the Royal Society, with the following inscription — "Invented by Sir Isaac Newton and made with his own hands, 1671."

There was at that time very little exact knowledge in Astronomy. All telescopes were tiny toys. The one which Newton invented was six inches long. No one, in Newton's generation, had any conception of the 100-ton telescopes which we have to-day.

Galileo had died one year before Newton was born. Forty-two years before Newton was born, Bruno had been burned to death in Rome for asserting that the earth moved around the sun.

So Newton found himself in the early days of astronomy, when it was even dangerous to think about such things.

It was when he was twenty-four years of age that he first conceived of the attraction of gravitation. He was sitting alone in his mother's garden, in the little farm village where he was born, when he saw the apple fall.

Why did it fall? What would be the weight

of that apple on an earth that was twice as large as ours? What would happen to the apple if it were halfway between the earth and the sun?

These were the questions he asked himself. He applied to this problem the full power of his mathematical mind.

He studied this problem for twenty years. Finally, he found out that the force of gravity and the centrifugal force balance each other. At last he had discovered the secret of the order of the heavens.

In 1687, when he was forty-five years old, he published his great book "The Principia." This book announced the principle of UNIVERSAL GRAVITATION.

This principle is that EVERY PARTICLE OF MATTER IN THE UNIVERSE IS ATTRACTED BY EVERY OTHER PARTICLE OF MATTER, WITH A FORCE INVERSELY PROPORTIONAL TO THE SQUARE OF THEIR DISTANCES.

Newton found out that the stone moves to the earth and that the earth moves to the stone. The sun is drawn to the earth, and the earth is drawn to the sun. Every atom is drawn to every other atom.

He discovered that what we call "weight" is a delusion. A man who weighs 150 pounds on the earth, for instance, would weigh two tons if he were on the sun.

Newton never at any time tried to keep his inventions and discoveries secret. He freely told them to his friends. The result was that in several instances other people claimed his inventions as their own.

Liebnitz, for instance, a German, claimed to have invented Fluxions. But it has been proved that Newton invented Fluxions at least ten years before Liebnitz.

The greatest trouble that Newton ever had was when he had finished a book on "The Nature of Light." He had worked on it for twenty years. Then, while he was absent from his study, his little dog overturned a candle which set fire to his book and destroyed it.

It is said that when Newton entered the room and saw what had been done he exclaimed: "Oh, Diamond, Diamond, little do you know the mischief you have done!"

In his later years, Newton went into public life. He became a Member of Parliament. He was appointed Master of the Mint. Queen Anne conferred upon him the honor of knighthood. Better still, he became the President of the Royal Society.

In 1727, when he was eighty-five years old, he died. His body was conveyed to Westminster Abbey, where it lies near the entrance to the choir on the left-hand side.

Happily, he died honored and rich. His personal estate was worth about $160,000. And his fame has grown more and more through the centuries.

He was a modest, candid and sociable man. He had no vanity. He was fond of people as well as of principles.

A short time before his death he uttered this memorable sentiment: "I do not know what I may appear to the world; but to myself I seem to have been only like a boy playing on the seashore, and diverting myself by now and then finding a smoother pebble or a prettier shell, whilst the great ocean of Truth lay all undiscovered before me."

WILLIAM PITT

WILLIAM PITT was born in 1759. If ever a statesman was born great, he was. His father was Lord Chatham, and his mother was a Grenville. He was born and bred in statesmanship.

He had every advantage except health. All his life he was more or less of an invalid. He was tortured by headaches and dyspepsia and gout.

He graduated at Cambridge when he was only seventeen. He was an amazing student, with a passion for knowledge and discussion. His brain had been quickened and developed by daily conversations with his father, who was his counsellor in all matters.

Pitt was from his earliest days a man of books, and at twenty he was given a book that shaped his whole policy and career. It was the ONE BOOK of his life — "WEALTH OF NATIONS," by Adam Smith.

This book was the Magna Charta of trade and commerce. It was not interesting. It was full of facts, figures and logic. No other statesman of the day had enough intelligence or patience to read it.

But Pitt did. It taught him the evil of State Control. It proved to him that BUSINESS MUST BE FREE.

Once a public dinner was given to Adam Smith. He arrived late, after all were seated. The diners all rose to their feet as he entered, and Pitt exclaimed gaily — "We will stand till you are seated, for we are all your scholars."

At twenty Pitt went to Lincoln's Inn to study law. He was obliged to support himself, as his income from his father's estate was only $1,250 a year.

At twenty-one he ran for Parliament and was badly defeated. But at twenty-two he was given a seat by Lord Lonsdale, who had nine "Pocket Boroughs" to dispose of.

Pitt's first speech in Parliament was a plea for economy. His second speech was in favor of controlling the spending departments that were wasting the money of the nation.

He entered Parliament in the Black Year — 1781. Cornwallis had surrendered to the Americans. The sun of England's glory was eclipsed. A mad German King was breaking the British Empire apart.

WILLIAM PITT

At twenty-three Pitt became Chancellor of the Exchequer; and at twenty-four he was offered the position of Prime Minister at the head of a blundering Coalition. He refused it. Several months later the Coalition fell, and Pitt became Prime Minister with a free hand.

At first, Parliament laughed. "He will be Premier for a day," said the M.P.'s. HE WAS PREMIER FOR SEVENTEEN YEARS WITHOUT A BREAK.

His first Bill was for the "Reform of Abuses in the Public Offices." He attacked the Spenders.

Pitt was defeated by Parliament. But he refused to resign. The City of London and the East India Company came to his support. Pitt hung on until he had the nation behind him. Then he had a General Election, and came back to Parliament with a solid majority.

There was an "old gang." They opposed Pitt. They jeered at him, and he fought back. He appealed straight to the people and the people kept him Prime Minister for seventeen years.

The people were sick of the "old gang." They wanted some one who had courage to cast the money-spenders out of the temple of Government. They chose Pitt, and he saved England.

At first he was only twenty-four — a tall, angular, shy young man. He was stiff and dignified, except with his friends. He was plain-looking, except for his eyes, which were keen and piercing. He had an odd, uptilted nose and, a "d——d long, obstinate face," as King George III said.

Against him were Fox — one of the ablest debaters that Parliament has ever had; Sheridan and Burke — greatest of Irish orators; Grenville, Shelburne and Lord North — all veteran politicians of the "Squandermania" species.

Pitt fought them all. He even fought the King at times. He had a policy and he carried it out. He established his sinking fund to pay off the war debt. He levied higher taxes, but mostly on luxuries such as silk, horses, gold and silver plate, etc.

HE LOCKED THE TREASURY AGAINST THE SPENDING DEPARTMENTS. He said: "We must spend only what we can afford. Our first duty is to pay our debts and restore our trade and commerce."

In managing his own personal finances Pitt was a failure. He was in debt all his life, and

WILLIAM PITT

when he died Parliament voted $200,000 to pay his debts.

He cared for neither money nor rank. He was "Mr." Pitt to the end of his life. Once the merchants of London met and voted him a gift of $500,000, and he refused it.

His one object was to help his country, not himself. He was a nation-BUILDER, not a nation-WRECKER. He became a great statesman by SAVING the public money, not by spending it.

As long as he could he kept England out of the French Revolution. He reformed Parliament. He pushed the bureaucrats back into their places. He set business men free. And in 1792 he delivered his greatest speech against the slave trade and abolished it.

He tried to help Ireland and Russia, but he burnt his fingers. In the end, he had to fight Napoleon, but he avoided war until he had restored England to solvency and prosperity. He did not heap new wars and new taxes upon a weary and wounded nation. IN SIX YEARS HIS POLICY DOUBLED BRITISH EXPORTS.

Eventually he was dragged into war. His armies were usually beaten, as they were led by incompetent dukes; but his navy was victorious, because it had Nelson. For years, Nelson was Pitt's only comfort.

To raise money for war Pitt asked for voluntary contributions. He received a large amount. HE AND HIS FELLOW-MINISTERS GAVE ONE-FIFTH OF THEIR SALARIES. They were a higher breed, you see, in those days, than the sort of salary-lovers that we have to-day.

The continued successes of Napoleon worried Pitt and broke his health. The defeat at Austerlitz and the death of Nelson were more than he could endure. In 1806 he died. His last words were: "Oh, my country. How I love my country!"

Pitt never married. He loved a girl once and lost her. He had only one thought all his life — the prosperity of his own land. He was honest, strong, competent and courageous. He was called "The Pilot who weathered the storm."

CECIL RHODES

THIS is the story of a real STATESMAN — a man who increased the PROFITS, not the taxes, of his country — a man who was too purposeful and efficient to be appreciated by his generation.

I refer to CECIL RHODES — who put Central Africa into the British Empire.

Cecil Rhodes gave Britain Rhodesia. He gave her the central ridge of Africa, which controls the continent.

He gave her 700,000 square miles more land under British rule. He gave her a new province six times larger than Great Britain — three and a half times larger than France.

"And what are you doing in Africa, Mr. Rhodes?" asked Queen Victoria. "Extending your Majesty's dominions, Madam," replied Rhodes.

Cecil Rhodes was born in 1853, in a little English vicarage. His father was a parson.

The chicks were too many for the nest. There were nine sons and two daughters. So young Cecil, at seventeen, went to South Africa to join his elder brother on a small cotton farm. He made the voyage on a sailing vessel, which reached Cape Town, by great perseverance, in seventy days.

The following year he set out, with an oxcart, for Kimberley, where diamonds had just been discovered. He became a digger.

In two years he had made several thousand dollars. It was his first money. He decided to spend it all on a better education.

He returned and entered Oxford — a tall, lanky, shy youth, who was much more successful at sports than at his studies.

When he was twenty-one, an English doctor told him his heart and lungs were weak. "You have six months to live," said the doctor.

Rhodes fled for his life to Africa and lived for twenty-eight years. Better still, he lived the most resultful life of any one in the Victorian period. He packed his twenty-eight years with THINGS DONE.

He had three main purposes —

(1) To make money, because money is power.

(2) To develop and civilize Central Africa.

(3) To organize and extend the British Empire.

In a few years he became rich. He founded

the great De Beers Company in 1880, and extended it until it became one of the greatest companies in the world.

At thirty-five Rhodes was the "Diamond King."

Having enough money, he plunged into public life. He became a member of the Cape Parliament; and his first speech was in defense of the rights of the natives. At thirty-seven he was Prime Minister, and sat at his desk, in his shirt sleeves, administering the troubled affairs of the little colony.

In 1888 he made a bargain with Lobengula, the King of Mashonaland. He acquired all the mining rights in a territory as vast as Central Europe. He took possession with a small band of 1,000 men.

He founded RHODESIA and made it as British as Oxford or Lancashire.

Then came the famous Jameson Raid. Too much fuss has been made about this Raid. Unfortunately it failed. If there had been a few more like Rhodes and Jameson and Phillips, it would not have failed; and the tragedy of the Boer War might have been prevented.

Africa at that time was a land of raids. Everybody raided. The Boers did. The natives did. It was not a land of etiquette and decorum and Civil Service. It was a land of savages, in which a few strong men were battling for control.

The struggle, mainly, was between Kruger and Rhodes — the two strongest personalities that Africa has ever produced. Kruger was narrow. Rhodes, on the contrary, was broad. He saw Africa as part of the great wide world; and he wanted it free and prosperous.

Then came the crash of the Boer War. Cheered on by promises of support from the Kaiser, the Boers plunged against the British.

Rhodes went to Kimberley and took charge during the siege. He kept the town together and saved it. He lived just long enough to see the British flag everywhere — then he went to one of his favorite little cottages, lay down, sent for Jameson and died. His last words were — "So much to do, so little done."

According to his wish, he lies in a lonely grave, high on one of his African mountains. There is no word of praise on his grave-stone — nothing but the words — "Here lies Cecil John Rhodes." But it is a grave that will be a Mecca to South Africans as long as the world lasts.

Rhodes was a man of the simplest habits. He

wanted little for himself. At first he lived in a hut. He had all the instincts of a Boy Scout.

He dressed roughly. He preferred to have his aim straight and his tie crooked, than *vice versa*. When he was presented to the Sultan of Turkey, he had no frock coat to put on, and went in wearing his jacket.

Once, on shipboard, he had to go to bed while a kindly sailor put a sailcloth patch on his only pair of trousers.

He had steel-blue eyes and a hearty laugh. He had no patience with fools and snobs; but he was fond of the Boers, the natives, the settlers, and all practical, useful people.

On perilous occasions he could be as terrible as an African storm; but he was never angry over small matters.

He cared nothing for high-sounding phrases and schemes on paper. He was an optimist without the mist. He never fooled himself with words.

He was not a money-grabber. He kept no books. He was careless about money and seldom had any in his pocket. He kept his shares in coat pockets and odd drawers.

He was recklessly generous. Once, in a bad year, he gave $80,000 to the settlers in Rhodesia.

At the close of his life he built a large house for himself, but used it mainly as a hotel for all comers. "This place belongs as much to the public as to me," he said.

His favorite books were Plutarch's "LIVES," Gibbon's "DECLINE AND FALL," and the "MEDITATIONS" of Marcus Aurelius.

He was a man of great personal courage. He mastered men by his fearlessness and his will. Once he walked unarmed up to 500 armed natives and compelled them to make peace.

He loved the rough pioneer camps and he detested society. The only unhappy period in his life was when he was lionized in London. He despised soft, lazy people — "loafers," he called them.

When he was twenty-four he made a will — the most extraordinary will that any young man of twenty-four ever made. He left all his money to establish a "Secret Society" to extend British rule thoughout the world — to win back the States — to take Africa and South America and Asia under the one flag — to give Home Rule to all parts of the Empire and to link all together in an Imperial Parliament.

What was his object? Not conquest. Not mere Empire-building. No. His purpose was

TO RENDER WARS IMPOSSIBLE AND TO PROMOTE THE BEST INTERESTS OF THE HUMAN RACE.

Such was his conception of a League of Nations.

Rhodes abhorred bureaucracy. He did not believe that great work could be done by small men. He believed in breed and efficiency and human nature.

He established a wonderful system of scholarships, partly to broaden Oxford out of its narrow rut, and partly to link together the English speaking races.

LORD RHONDDA

THIS is the tale of D. A. THOMAS, known in the last two years of his life as LORD RHONDDA.

"D. A.," as his friends called him, was the greatest Business Builder that Wales has ever produced.

He was the creator of the "Cambrian Coal Combine" — a garden city of 12,000 well-paid miners. He built more than thirty companies and whatever he touched prospered.

When he died in 1918, he was worth $3,425,-000; but he might have had twice as much. He was always more intent on building a business than on getting his share of the profits.

D. A. Thomas was a merchant adventurer of the sort that built up the British Empire. He was more than that — he was an INDEPENDENT THINKER.

He was so independent that he has not yet been appreciated at his full worth.

He was born in a tiny Welsh village whose name I cannot spell. His father was a grocer who had gone into the coal trade and was sorry for it.

It is said that his father was standing at the pit-head, feeling very depressed over his losses, when a neighbor came to him with the news — "It's a boy."

"Well," said the father, "I don't know what is to become of him. There is only the workhouse in front of us."

Young D. A. was, at first, a delicate boy, but he trained himself into an athlete. He became a good walker, swimmer and cyclist. He was a clever boxer, too, and became the middle-weight champion of Cambridge, in spite of his bad eyesight.

He was always courageous. As a lad he won the medal of the Royal Humane Society for saving a man's life. He jumped into an icy lake and pulled him out.

At twenty-one his father died and he went into business. At twenty-six he married Sybil Haig, the daughter of a coal owner. They had one child — the present Viscountess Rhondda, who is now in control of her father's vast interests.

D. A. Thomas went into politics as well as business. He was a free trader.

As a politician he was a failure; or rather, he

was not the sort of man to succeed in the slippery trickeries of Parliament.

He was INDEPENDENT. That is the word that needs to be stressed in these days of human cogs.

The artful dodgers of politics feared and disliked him. He was too able — too honest — too fearless to be a member of the Government.

He was entirely neglected by the makers of Cabinets, just as Leverhulme was. It is a startling fact that D. A. Thomas sat in Parliament for twenty-five years and was never given any important office.

In 1910 he gave up politics. He realized he was quite unqualified to play the political game. He was not a good speaker. His voice was weak and he had never thought of training it.

He always preferred business to politics. Business was his life. He loved the excitement of it and the usefulness of it. He was a constant reader of business books.

He was not a looker-on. He was energy — all action. He liked his big desk in his big office in Cardiff.

He had a will like steel, but he was not a bully or a shouter. He was a quiet, tense, shrewd man, who seemed to foresee everything.

He had strikes, of course. No one can employ the miners of South Wales without having strikes. But even the strike leaders respected and liked D. A. once the battle was over.

All his life he resisted State Control. He opposed the State idea of a fixed wage to good and bad alike.

He had plenty of enemies — men who had tried to fool him, cheat him or threaten him. "No man is worth his salt," he said, "who has no enemies."

He despised slackers and tricksters and unreliable people. He was not an idealist. He knew what human nature is. But he was all for fair play and the rules of the game.

When he became wealthy his money did not spoil him. He never became a Nabob. He was always companionable. He liked workmen and he preferred a colliery at any time to the House of Lords.

He was fond of farming, though he could never make it pay. Who can? He had a large herd of Herefords and a great country estate.

During the War he threw his private affairs on one side and gave all his energies to the Government.

He and his daughter went down on the

Lusitania but were picked up and saved. No sooner was he in England than he was asked to cross the ocean again, and he went. He was a man without fear.

As a Food Controller he succeeded as no other Food Controller in any country did. Every one felt that he was fair and that what he was doing was right.

At last, in 1918, his war burdens crushed him, and he died — twenty years too soon. He gave his life for his country.

He was a typically British business man of the highest type.

He loved Wales, miners and all. He took his title from the Rhondda Valley, where his miners lived. And he showered all manner of gifts on Cardiff.

CHARLES SEABROOK

CHARLIE SEABROOK! No, you have never heard of him. He is not famous yet. He has just started.

He is only forty-three years old, but he is THE MOST EFFICIENT FARMER IN THE WORLD.

IN ONE YEAR HE RAISED VEGETABLES WORTH $500,000 ON A FARM OF 1,200 ACRES.

He runs his farm on factory lines. He is not a farmer, in the ordinary sense. He doesn't chuck his seed in the ground and let Nature and the birds do the rest.

HE IS A MANUFACTURER OF VEGETABLES; and he gets a greater output per acre than any one else ever did.

Now that we are all talking about OUTPUT, this story shows how to get it. No matter whether we are in an office, or a factory, or on a farm, the general principles of production are the same.

The story of Charlie Seabrook began with his birth in 1883, on a small farm in Bridgeton, New Jersey. His father was not very successful as a farmer.

Charlie began to work at five years of age. At fourteen he was doing the work of a man.

He was a hard worker, but he was not fond of sweat and dirt and drudgery. He toiled because he thought he must, but as he worked he thought, Is there no better, quicker, easier way to operate a farm?

He was fond of books and magazines. He bought every good book on farming that he could afford.

He was a READER and a THINKER — that was the beginning of his success.

At twenty-five he had three definite ideas:

(1) The farm needs more rain.
(2) The farm needs more manure.
(3) One crop a year is not enough.

He began by putting up an overhead irrigation system. He ran a $1\frac{1}{4}$-inch iron pipe on top of six-foot posts. The pipe was perforated, so as to throw out a fine spray. The pipes were placed fifty feet apart. He tried this on three acres, and the results were wonderful.

Thus, he improved on Nature. He created ARTIFICIAL RAIN.

Until he was twenty-five, Charlie Seabrook worked for his father; after that age his father worked for Charlie. He was a wise father.

In 1911 the two Seabrooks made a profit of $25,000. "Now let us put it in the bank," said the father.

"No," said Charlie, "let us put it back into the LAND. The land is the best bank."

They put it into the land. They almost squandered it on the land. The near-by farmers thought they were mad.

"Make a dollar and then put it back to make more dollars" — is one of the principles Charlie Seabrook learned from his books.

He saw the value of FERTILIZATION, as few farmers do. He discovered that soil had to be made.

Ordinary soil is not really soil at all, any more than four wheels and a gear-box are a motor-car. It is only a start — a place for your crops to stand on.

So, young Seabrook began to make soil. He put 100 TONS OF MANURE PER ACRE on new land; and forty tons on old land. Then he put two or three tons of bone meal per acre at $60 a ton on top of the 100 tons.

A hundred tons per acre! At $2.50 a ton! $370 per acre — just for fertilization! No wonder the other farmers jeered at Seabrook and his book learning.

On top of this came the cost of irrigation — $300 per acre. The first cost of the land was not less than $150 per acre, so that the total cost for just one acre was:

First cost	$150
Irrigation	300
Fertilization	370
Total	$820

The Seabrook farm was a joke until the next year, when the amazing story was told by the village grocer that Charlie Seabrook made more than $2,000 on a single acre. Since then the other farmers have stopped making jokes. They don't understand what has happened, but they wish they did.

Just to show what Seabrook actually did, here is a page out of his farm ledger, telling what was done on a single acre:

"Planted in spinach, Feb. 25. Spinach sold Ap. 15 for $150. Planted potatoes May 10. Potatoes sold Aug. 10 for $450. Romanie planted Aug. 11, intercropped with strawberries. Romanie sold Oct. for $500. Total sales, $1,100.

"Second year. A half-crop of strawberries, sold for $600.

"Third year. One crop of strawberries,

$1,300. One crop of lettuce, $1,000. One crop of spinach, $150. Total sales $2,450."

This is an average of $1,385 per acre. The gross profit was therefore about $650 per acre.

Seabrook gets three crops a year — sometimes FOUR. For instance, he has had crops of spinach, potatoes, lettuce and spinach from the same land in one year.

He has had 604 bushels of potatoes in one crop from one acre. He has had 8,500 quarts of strawberries from one acre.

His specialty is lettuce, for the reason that he has found it to be the most profitable. Here are a few of his sales in one year:

Lettuce	$112,050
Cabbage	39,245
Radishes	36,800
Spinach	31,970
Onions	24,770
Potatoes	21,760
Strawberries	18,905
Cucumbers	17,545

Charlie Seabrook now has 1,200 acres, but nearly all of his output has come from 200 acres. He has organized his farm into a stock company. It has $500,000 of paid-up capital. And it makes 20 per cent profits.

There are 300 workers on this farm; and in berry-picking time there are twice as many. The workers live on the farm in neat concrete houses. They work ten hours a day, all the year, and are paid weekly.

If you ask — "What do they do in the winter?" the answer is — "There is no winter on the Seabrook Farm."

There are six enormous greenhouses, each 60 by 300 feet. These cost over $10,000 apiece, and at first they were called "Seabrook's Folly."

These greenhouses give Seabrook a LONGER YEAR. They abolish winter. They enable him to grow vegetables out of season, at top prices. He intends to build more greenhouses.

Then, in the winter, the workers go into a box factory on the farm, and make 100,000 boxes for their own use.

The farm has a large office, too, with its typewriters, comptometers and filing cabinets.

There is a cold storage warehouse, 60 by 325 feet in size; a garage for the four tractors and the eight wagons; a stable for fifty horses; a machine-shop for making repairs; and a railway siding.

"This is not a farm," says Seabrook. "It is a FOOD-FACTORY.

FRED SELOUS

IN 1920 a noble statue of Fred Selous was unveiled in the South Kensington Museum, London, in the midst of his trophies of the jungle. He is surrounded by elephant tusks, moose antlers, buffalo horns and lion heads.

He was one of the greatest lion-hunters who ever lived. He shot thirty-one lions, two hundred buffaloes and no one knows how many elephants.

For forty years he earned his living with his rifle and his courage in the wildest parts of Africa, America, Canada, and Alaska. He was the hero of a thousand hairbreadth escapes. He preferred danger to safety, and he lived in danger all his life.

Fred Selous was born in 1851, in a London home near the Zoo. His full name was Frederick Courtney Selous. His father was the chairman of the Stock Exchange.

His mother was a great reader of Scott's tales of adventure and told them to her children.

These tales made a deep impression on him

and from the first he wanted to be a hunter of wild animals.

At school he was the despair of his teachers. He was always in trouble. One teacher said of him: "He breaks every rule. He climbs out of the window to go bird-nesting. He is constantly complained of for trespassing. He locked one of the teachers in a cowshed. He is the plague of our lives."

One night, when he was twelve years old, a teacher found him lying in his nightshirt on the bare floor of his room. He explained: "Well, you see, one day I'm going to be a hunter in Africa, and I'm just hardening myself so that I can sleep on the ground."

At seventeen he left school and began to travel. He tried to be a doctor, but soon gave it up and went to Africa. He landed at Algoa Bay with $2,000. He became a hunter of big game at eighteen.

He made his way at once into the interior of Africa. He went straight to Lobengula, the king of the Matabeles. "I want your permission to hunt elephants," he said.

Lobengula laughed. "Don't you mean rabbits?" he asked. "You're nothing but a boy."

"I'm going to hunt elephants," said young

Fred Selous. Lobengula snorted with contempt. "Go wherever you like, " he said. "You are of no consequence."

Several weeks later, Fred Selous came back with 450 lbs. of ivory and a profit of $1,500. Lobengula was amazed. "Why, you're not a boy," he said, "you're a man. You must now take a wife."

Many years afterwards, when the Matabeles attacked the British, it was Fred Selous who led the British soldiers against Lobengula and drove the old King into exile. The "boy" dethroned the King and added another province to the British Empire.

It was Selous, too, who told Cecil Rhodes about Mashonaland. He made the first road through the African jungle. It has always been called the "Selous Road."

Although he returned frequently to England, Fred Selous spent almost his entire life in the wild places of the earth. He made his life an endless adventure. He despised safety and comfort.

Fred Selous was not a mere slaughterer of wild animals. He hunted for trade and for science. He was a naturalist above all else. He was just as keen to catch a new butterfly as he was to kill a lion. He never killed an animal except for a definite purpose.

He was always willing to run risks. He hunted often with poor guns, and one gave him a scar that he carried for life. His best gun was a 450 single shot.

He had a will like steel. Nothing could turn him aside. The higher the obstacle, the higher his heart.

He was a constant reader. His favorite authors were Dickens, Byron and Hardy. He was an author himself, too. His best books, perhaps, are "A Hunter's Wanderings," and "African Nature Notes."

He was a wonderful story-teller when among friends. He had a rich, resonant voice and he was never at a loss for a word. He was one of the few men in the world that Theodore Roosevelt loved to listen to.

He was modest about his own exploits. "Just because I have hunted a lot," he said, "that is not to say I am a specially good hunter." He never bragged. He made less fuss over the thirty-one lions he had shot than some men do over a couple of rabbits.

He was a simple, boyish man. He hated lawyers, politicians, professors and society people. He was full of fun. He was a true Peter Pan. He was the ideal of all Boy Scouts.

Although he lived most of his life among savages and wild animals he was always tender and refined. He was not a cynic.

He loved sport. He was a good cricketer. He rode a horse well. He was fond of cycling. Once, when he was fifty-seven, he cycled 100 miles.

His senses were remarkably acute. He could see and hear as well as a Red Indian. He had developed a most unusual power of observation.

He lived simply and had perfect health. He drank nothing but tea — tea and plenty of it. His favorite meal, he said, was "good fat moose and tea." At sixty-three he was straight, strong and handsome. His eyes were as clear and blue as the sky.

When the World War broke out, he ran to the War Office and offered himself but was told, "You're too old."

He persevered, and at last was sent to East Africa. Of all the officers in his regiment, he was the only one who kept out of the hospital. He won his D. S. O. He was made a major. He led his men well, and then in a battle with Germans he was shot by a sniper. He was sewn up in a blanket and buried in a nameless spot in the wild jungle he loved.

HE WAS THE SIR GALAHAD OF AFRICA. HE WAS THE "HAPPY WARRIOR." HE DID AS MUCH AS ANY MAN TO TEACH AFRICA THE BRITISH CODE OF JUSTICE, TRUTHFULNESS, COURAGE AND FAIR PLAY.

SIR SWIRE SMITH

THE best way to judge a man's success in life is by the size of his funeral. It is a final demonstration of his power to make friends.

So, by this test, Sir Swire Smith was successful. At his funeral more than 700 mourners marched behind the hearse, while thousands lined the streets. He had lived seventy-six years, as men count time, and in the quality of his life he was one of the top men of his generation.

Sir Swire Smith was a MASTER SPINNER. Also, he was a SPORT — a WIT — a SINGER — a TRAVELER — an EDUCATOR — a PAL — a PIONEER.

He was the Peter Pan of Yorkshire. He was younger at seventy-six than most men are at thirty.

He was born in 1842 in a small cottage in Keighley, which stands at the top of England in technical education and in the buying of War Bonds, largely through the efforts of Swire Smith. His father had a little machine shop. He was a Methodist, and young Swire was reared under the strictest of John Wesley's rules.

He was a merry boy, with blue eyes and wavy hair. He was full of mischief, as most normal boys are. At sixteen he went to work in a spinning mill.

At twenty he started on his own as a spinner of wool, with a capital of $1,800. He did not succeed very well, as he was never at any time a keen money-maker. The wool trade was dull and full of uncertainties.

Swire Smith did not find himself until he was twenty-five. Then he heard a lecture by Samuel Smiles, the author of "Self Help."

At that time Samuel Smiles was going up and down England and Scotland, writing and lecturing on efficiency and the need of technical education. He was a voice crying in the wilderness. He was warning Britain that Germany and America were coming to the front.

Swire Smith was set on fire by this lecture. At once he became the secretary of the Mechanics' Institute.

There were only 20,000 people in Keighley at that time, and few cared a button for technical education, but young Swire made them pay up. He raised $55,000 for a technical school. In 1870 it was opened.

Its purpose was to apply the principles of

science and art to the activities of trade and commerce. Keighley led the way, but Britain did not follow. If she had, she would be in a much happier position to-day.

That little school in Keighley produced Northrop — the inventor of the automatic loom. It produced W. H. Watkinson, of the "hush-hush" boats; and Alfred Fowler, of the Royal College of Science.

It stirred up Parliament, and the result was the Technical Instruction Act of 1889. This Act spent millions of pounds on similar schools. By this time the Keighley school was leading the way with 1,400 students.

Keighley started the United States, too, as well as Britain. Andrew Carnegie, who was a lifelong friend of Swire Smith, visited Keighley, saw the school, and promptly went back to Pittsburgh and built the largest technical school in America.

All this, you see, sprang from the enthusiasm of a young man of twenty-five, who had heard a lecture on Efficiency by Samuel Smiles.

When he was thirty-nine, Swire Smith persuaded the Government to appoint a Royal Commission on Technical Instruction. He and six others were appointed.

This Commission went to Germany and discovered many startling facts. They found 8,000 students in staff training schools in Hamburg. They found that Stuttgart, a small town, had more students than Liverpool.

They went to France, Switzerland, America and Canada, and their report started a progressive movement in most British industries. This report, as the Government admitted, was "largely compiled from the notes of Sir Swire Smith."

As an employer, Sir Swire Smith set a good example. His plan was "to get the best hands by paying top wages." He started staff training in his own mill, and paid half the fees of any worker who wanted a better education.

He went through his mill twice a day, when he was at home. He knew all his workers by name and took lunch with them in a canteen.

Once he was delighted when a small boy in the street said to another boy, "See yon man! He works at our mill."

Swire Smith believed in "fun and forty per cent," but he was fonder of the fun than the forty. His creed was, "If your business interferes with happiness, better give up your business."

As a story-teller he had few superiors. Wherever he was there was laughter. His tales were never at an end.

He had a very fine baritone voice, and was always ready to sing an old ballad or a scrap of an opera.

As a speaker he was breezy, entertaining and practical. He had no starch in him. Honors did not sober him. He was a boy to the last — just before he died he learned a new dance and wrote amusing letters to a couple of kiddies.

He never married, though he was in love many times. He was never lonely. The world was his family.

Such was Sir Swire Smith, who was, as Will Crooks once said, "the pioneer of real education in Great Britain."

FREDERICK WINSLOW TAYLOR

THIS is the story of Taylor — Frederick Winslow Taylor, who was the originator of Industrial Efficiency.

Taylor was born in a suburb of Philadelphia in 1856. During the Civil War he was a small boy — too small to understand what the war was about.

His parents were neither rich nor poor. They were rich enough, however, to send young Fred Taylor to attend school in France. They planned to send him to Harvard University and educate him for a lawyer.

He was a good student. He studied so hard that he injured his eyes and at nineteen he was compelled by his bad eyesight to leave school. THIS SERIOUS BLOW WAS THE MAKING OF HIM.

He went out and secured a job as an apprentice in a tiny machine-shop near his home. He stayed three years. He learned to be a machinist. Also, he learned to be a pattern-maker.

When he was twenty-two he went to the Midvale Steel Works and got a job as a laborer. But he was not a laborer very long.

First, he was gang boss over the lathe hands.

Second, he was Assistant Foreman of the Machine-shop.

Third, he was Foreman.

Fourth, he was master mechanic in charge of repairs and maintenance.

Fifth, he was Chief Draughtsman.

Sixth, he was Chief Engineer.

He climbed up from Laborer to Chief Engineer in six years. During this time his eyesight improved and he took the Engineering Course at Stevens' Institute, studying at nights and on Sundays. It was while he was foreman, at the age of twenty-three, that he first began to apply Scientific methods to manufacturing.

He invented a new art of cutting metals with high-speed steel, by means of which a cutting tool is now able to do three times as much.

He made tens of thousands of experiments. He was a man of the greatest patience and perseverance.

He received a share in his inventions and in 1901 he retired from money-making. As he said: "I can no longer afford to work for money."

Taylor was not a genius. He was not brilliant. He was not adaptable. Perhaps the secret of his success was his mastery of himself. He had the most dogged persistence that ever man had.

Once he began a job, nothing could make him quit until he had finished it. As he once admitted, his success was due to holding on with his teeth.

Once, when he was defining his idea of Character, he called it "the ability to do disagreeable things."

Taylor believed that if a man only did what he liked to do he was a mere trifler. The main thing is to do what NEEDS to be done whether you like to do it or not.

For instance, Taylor once forced himself to learn bookkeeping, although he detested it, because he found that efficient accounting is of such importance to a manufacturer.

Taylor made himself the SERVANT OF HIS JOB. He devoted himself with the greatest zeal and the most tireless patience to the common, every-day work which most people neglect — that is, in short, the secret of his success.

Taylor was a DOER. He was not an original thinker in the sense that Herbert Spencer was. He had little imagination and not very much tact. He was absolutely simple and straightforward.

If he came to a difficulty he never once thought of dodging it or walking around it. He went AT it. He went through it or over it. He deliberately all through life followed the line of MOST resistance.

Taylor cared nothing for social life. He never wished to be ornamental or entertaining. He cared much less for people than for facts. He was a devotee of facts.

Taylor would not go out of his way one inch to please public opinion. He was the exact opposite of a politician. He cared nothing for opinions, not even for his own. His one aim was to FIND OUT WHAT OUGHT TO BE DONE.

Taylor never tried to make a smooth path for himself or his methods. He worked ceaselessly to learn what he knew; and once he had discovered a fact he held fast to it.

He made himself rich. Better still, he made his Company rich. And still better, HE RECONSTRUCTED THE MACHINE-SHOPS OF THE WORLD.

Taylor was not a genius. At any rate, he always denied vigorously that he was. He always said that he had no especial ability — just grit and common sense. He owed his success, in his own opinion, to what he called "PLAIN EVERYDAY PERSISTENCE."

In his later life Taylor was a TEACHER of men. But in his earlier life he was a LEARNER. He was always getting instruction from books and older men and personal experiments.

As a young man, he got quick promotion by his willingness to work overtime, and by the care he took of his machines. The managers soon took notice of him, and he was in demand.

Taylor was greatly impressed by some advice he received from an old manufacturer. The old gentleman noticed him, as an apprentice, and sent for him. He said to Taylor: "If you want to succeed in life, I will tell you how to do it. If your employer wants you to start work at 7 o'clock in the morning, always be there at ten minutes before seven. If he wants you to stay until 6 o'clock at night, always stay until ten minutes past six. If you haven't sense enough to know what I mean by this, you haven't sense enough to succeed, anyway."

One morning, when Taylor was a foreman, a valve broke. It compelled the whole department to shut down. Taylor went all over Philadelphia to get a valve. He went to every dealer in the city. He failed. There were none.

He came back to the works, went to the General Manager and began to tell how thoroughly he had hunted for a valve. The General Manager glared at him.

"Do you mean to tell me that you haven't got that valve?"

"Yes, sir."

"Get out of this," roared the Manager, "AND GET THAT VALVE."

Taylor went to New York — ninety miles — and got the valve. This event taught him an important lesson. As he used to say: "That was when I learned not to offer reasons instead of results."

On another occasion he was much impressed by a remark made in 1876 by "Old Man Sharpe," of the famous Brown and Sharpe Works. Sharpe asked him: "What is your idea of Success?"

"Oh," said Taylor, "I want to be a machinist and to earn $2.50 a day."

"No," said Sharpe, "that is not enough to aim at. When I was your age I decided that I would learn how to do work just a little more ACCURATELY than anybody else, and always to do better work this year than I did last year."

For several years Taylor served under William Sellers, a famous engineer. One day he went to Sellers and complained that a certain ill-tempered manager had been treating him badly. He told his troubles to Sellers at some length. Sellers listened patiently and then replied:

"Do you know that all of this impresses me with the fact that you are still a very young man? Long before you reach my age, you will have found out that you have to eat a bushel of dirt, and you will go right ahead and eat it until it really seriously interferes with your digestion."

This reply was taken to heart by young Taylor; and he determined not to weaken his character by complaint and peevishness.

Once when he had climbed to be the Head of a small Department, a drain clogged up. This drain ran twenty-five feet deep under the factory. He sent a gang to clear it out. They worked at it with connecting rods and failed. They reported that it would have to be opened up.

This would stop the factory for several days; so Taylor decided to clear the drain himself. He took off his clothes, put on overalls, tied shoes on his elbows and knees, and crawled into the drain.

Several times he had to hold his nose high in the arch of the drain to keep from drowning. He crawled forward in the darkness over 100 yards. He found the obstruction, pulled it out of the way and backed out through the slime.

He was covered with dirt but victorious. His fellow-workers laughed at him, but the Chairman of the Company heard of it and told the story to the Directors. He had saved the Company many dollars. This secured him another promotion.

Taylor was a man of tremendous will power and independence. Above all, he was strong. No one could break him or bend him. Once he started to do a job, nobody could stop him.

He was rough. His language, when he was excited was too vividly personal and descriptive to be put into print. He swore. Once when a Parliamentary Committee reproved him for his language he said apologetically:

"I fear, gentlemen, that my early education was much neglected."

There was no make-believe about Taylor. He had no patience with fools; and he scorned all humbug as only a strong man can.

His mind was too large to worry about split infinitives. If he had a collar and tie on, very well; if not, what matter? He spent no time on trifles.

He was well born, in the highest sense. His

father's ancestors were English Friends, and his mother was descended from a Puritan family named Spooner, who went to America in the *Mayflower*.

But Taylor cared nothing for birth and very little for education. He had no swank of any sort. He preferred workmen to professors. He was always a natural and straightforward man, whom everybody respected, and a few people loved.

He had very little liking for either labor leaders or directors. Most of his life he fought both. One was as bad as the other, he thought, in preventing improvements.

He did not believe in coddling workmen. He thought that they should be treated fairly and left alone to do as they liked with their own lives.

In his day, welfare work was just beginning and making many mistakes. The most of it, in Taylor's opinion, was about as useful as putting ribbons on lathes.

Taylor worked WITH his men. He was not afraid of them. When they did wrong, he told them what he thought in a way that they never forgot. He was not an easy boss; but he was fair. He was always a man among men.

Even in his later life, when he was rich and

famous, he considered himself as a worker; and he was never so happy as when he had his greasy overalls on in the middle of his men.

He believed in high wages, but he believed in men being workers, not bandits. He said that it was the duty of a company to give its workers a fair chance to earn as much as possible; then, if a worker slacked and balked, let him go elsewhere.

Give the job fair play, and there will be plenty of money for all of us — that was his doctrine.

He despised laziness, trickery and swank as a trinity of evil. He weeded them out of every factory he worked in.

He made work a pleasure by putting his brains into it. He lifted work up to the level of science.

He never put money first. Once he said, "All our inventions are made to produce human happiness."

Workmen quit their jobs to go to his funeral. He was to them the greatest of leaders — he was "A WHITE MAN," they said.

In his last public address, made a few weeks before his death, he said — "We must always remember that the most important thing in any business is RIGHT RELATIONS."

Such was Fred Taylor — the founder of Industrial Efficiency. HE WAS EQUALLY GREAT AS A MAN AND AS A MASTER ENGINEER.

JAMES WATT

HERE is a story which every father should tell to his children — which every employer should tell to his workers — the inspiring story of JAMES WATT.

James Watt invented the steam engine. He created the age of Steam.

James Watt was born in Greenock, Scotland, in 1736. At that time there were no factories, railroads, steamships, machines, free schools, penny postage, or Free Trade.

He was a delicate boy. He had very little schooling. He was taught mainly by his mother.

He was a zealous reader of good books. At fifteen he had twice read "The Elements of Philosophy."

His father and grandfather were skilled mechanics; and so, when he was a boy, little "Jamie," as he was called, spent his time doing three things —

    (1) Making toy machinery.
    (2) Reading serious books.
    (3) Roaming the woods.

He was fond of making experiments; and

once he spent an hour studying the tea-kettle. He covered the spout to test the lifting power of steam. His aunt, who saw him doing this, told him that he was wasting his time playing with steam.

At seventeen, his mother died and his father suddenly became poor. James went to Glasgow and got a petty job mending spectacles, fishing rods, etc.

When he was nineteen he journeyed to London — ON HORSEBACK. This was the first Great Event of his life.

That was in 1755. The journey took twelve days. It was a very dangerous and uncomfortable journey.

Watt stayed in London. He worked in a small shop, making scientific instruments. Then he went back to Glasgow.

He was called in to mend the scientific instruments of Glasgow University. This was the second Great Event of his life.

Several professors appreciated Watt. They gave him a workroom in the University. Here Watt mended the apparatus of the University, and also made fishing tackle for outside customers. He even went so far as to make an improved organ.

When Watt was twenty-three came the third Great Event — he found an old model of a steam engine in the University. Of course it was not a practical steam-engine. It was one that would not work. But it fascinated Watt. He at once began to study steam.

He ran against a serious obstacle to begin with — most of the articles on steam were written in French and Italian. Very little was written in English. Watt at once began to study French and Italian, and persevered until he could read the articles on steam.

In 1764 he married a helpful wife. He was doing well in business. He had sixteen workmen and was making clear profits of $3,000 a year.

He was now thinking of steam and nothing else. In 1765 he wrote to a friend, "My whole thoughts are bent on this machine." He made a crude model. It would not work. He made a second one, and it would not work. And a third one, and a fourth one.

At that time there was no workshop in the world which could make a perfect cylinder. This made much trouble for Watt.

He neglected his business. He got into debt. Then came the fourth Great Event — he met

Dr. Roebuck, founder of the Carron Iron Works.

Dr. Roebuck was the first man who dared to invest money in steam. He gave Watt $5,000 to pay off the debts. In return Watt gave Dr. Roebuck a two-thirds interest in the steam engine.

Watt was never a business man. He hated buying and selling. He was an inventor — nothing else.

All the while he was in bad health. He had fits of despondency. He had headaches. But he persevered, and in 1769 he got his first patent.

On January 5th, 1769, Watt and Arkwright received patents for the first steam engine and the first spinning-machine.

Watt had now the right idea of a steam engine, but he could not get it made in any workshop. Model after model failed or acted badly. He had no proper packing, and had to use old hats and cork. All his models leaked. He could not find any workman who had enough skill to make the steam engine.

Then came more debts. His friend, Dr. Roebuck, went into bankruptcy. On top of it all his wife died. Then came the fifth Great Event — he met Matthew Boulton. This was in 1773.

Matthew Boulton had a model factory in Birmingham. He made clocks. He was one of the ablest business men and thinkers of his day.

He was a friend of Franklin and Wedgwood and Priestley. He was an organizer. He had a genius for business. He was a noble and competent man.

Dr. Roebuck owed Boulton $1,000 and Boulton took two-thirds of Watt's patent in payment. So in 1774 Watt and his engine moved from Glasgow to Birmingham. Everybody made fun of the engine all along the way as it traveled by wagon.

During this year Watt made $1,000 by surveying. He gave part of it to Dr. Roebuck. His own personal expenses were only $10 a week. He was offered $5,000 a year by the Russian Government. He was offered an easy Government job at Kronstadt; but he refused it. He stuck to Boulton and his engine.

At this point one of his workmen stole the drawings of the engine and sold it to another firm. The result was competition. For self-protection Watt had to get his patent extended for seven years. The great Burke, in Parliament, made a stately oration against this extension, but to no effect.

Then came the sixth Great Event. Watt met Wilkinson, who knew how to make good cylinders. At once the Watt steam engine became a practical machine.

Orders came in from collieries for pumping engines. Boulton gave orders to make sixty-five the first year. From this time onward the steam engine was a success.

In 1802 a friend wrote to Watt and said, "Why not steam instead of post horses? Why not an iron railroad?" This was the first suggestion ever made of a steam railroad.

The next year Fulton ordered an engine from Boulton and Watt, and in 1807 the first steamship ran on the Hudson River. By this time there were many competitors. There was much litigation. Watt and Boulton won these lawsuits, but they were very costly. One London lawyer charged a fee of $30,000.

Watt and Boulton were partners for twenty-five years. Then they retired, and the partnership was continued by their sons. Watt had two sons and Boulton one.

By 1824 Boulton and Watt had made 1,164 steam engines, with a horsepower of 25,945. To-day the horsepower of steam engines is equal to the strength of 4,500,000,000 men.

In his old age Watt was showered with honors. He had riches and praise. When he died in 1819, at Heathfield, in Staffordshire, he was known all over the civilized world.

In his memory a tablet was erected in Westminster Abbey. Lord Brougham wrote the inscription in noble words — "He enlarged the resources of his country. . . . He increased the power of man. . . ."

GEORGE WESTINGHOUSE

I INVITE you to spend five minutes in reading the story of George Westinghouse for the following reasons:

(1) He was an INVENTOR who built up a company with $60,000,000 assets.

(2) He was an EMPLOYER who had 50,000 workers who never went on strike.

(3) He was a MAN who became rich and famous, but who remained simple, friendly and useful to the last day of his life.

He died in 1914, and a remarkably interesting biography of him has been written by Francis E. Leupp.

Westinghouse was born poor, of course, as most great men are. His father was a sort of carpenter-farmer, in a tiny village.

He was born in 1846; and it is worth mentioning that for a year before his birth his father was engaged in the invention of a threshing machine. There were pre-natal influences that destined the baby boy to be a great inventor.

At school young George Westinghouse was a failure; at least, so the teacher said. He was a big, clumsy boy, a ready fighter and with a will and temper that made him uncontrollable.

He was always at the foot of the class; and his parents and the teacher wondered what would ever become of him. Like Darwin, Edison, Clive, and many others, he was an "ugly duckling" who grew up to be a swan.

Whenever he could he ran away from school and made engines out of wood with his jack-knife. Usually, his father caught him and smashed the engine.

At last, one of his father's workmen took pity on the boy and fitted up a little workshop in a hay-loft where his predatory father could not find George.

At fourteen he quit school and became a worker for his father for fifty cents a day. Even this amount was too much, so his father thought, as the lad spent his time trying to invent a machine to do his work.

"His one desire," said his puzzled father, "is to avoid work."

At seventeen he became a soldier in the Civil War. He joined the cavalry because he thought riding would be easier than walking; and he was greatly disappointed when he found he would have to care for his own horse.

At nineteen he went to college, but he felt as much out of place as a fish in a bag of feathers. "He was my despair," said one of the Professors. His brain craved creative work, not the memorizing of dead languages.

So, on the advice of the Head of the college, young Westinghouse went back home and became a mechanic. He worked for his father for $2 a day.

At twenty, very luckily, he was in a railway wreck. Two coaches jumped the track and the line was blocked for two hours.

At once he thought of an invention to put the cars on the track in half an hour. He patented this and actually found two men who bought a share in the patent for $5,000 apiece.

This was the beginning of his real career. From that moment, he spent his whole life in inventing improvements for railways.

At this time, too, he fell in love. He met a beautiful girl named Marguerite Walker in a railway coach — all his good fortune came from railways. He courted her and married her; and she became the inseparable partner of all his failures and successes.

She, in her own way, was fully as clever and original as he was himself. She was always more to him than all the world. She stood with him all through life and followed him quickly in death.

Soon after his marriage Westinghouse saw another railway wreck. Two trains had collided, head on. The track was level and straight. He asked why the collision had happened.

"The two engineers saw each other, but they couldn't stop," said the stationmaster. "They hadn't time. You can't stop a train in a moment."

Westinghouse still asked why. He studied the old-fashioned hand-brake system and found it was hopeless.

Some better way was needed, so that the driver could stop his own train. He studied this problem for months. He tried using a long chain, tightened by the driver, but it was too clumsy. He tried steam, but it was affected by heat and cold.

Then came a lucky accident. One morning a young woman came into his office, asking for subscriptions to a magazine called "The Living Age."

She asked Westinghouse. He refused rather roughly and she turned away sadly. He noticed that she was gentle and timid, and he regretted his roughness. He called her back and gave her $2.

"You may send me your magazine for a few months," he said.

Soon the first number came and Westinghouse, who had never been a reader, was surprised to find an article that solved the brake problem.

The article was entitled, "In the Mont Cenis Tunnel." It was written by an English engineer; and it told how the tunnel had been dug by the use of COMPRESSED AIR.

This engineer told how compressed air was carried 3,000 feet in a pipe and used to drive a drill through the solid rock of Mont Cenis.

Westinghouse shouted with joy. Here was the hint he had needed. If compressed air could be used to drive a drill, why could it not be used to operate the brakes of a train?

He threw everything else aside and hurled himself into the task of making the first air-brake. In a few weeks he had one finished. It worked. In a jiffy he had become one of the greatest inventors of the world.

Of course, he had the usual difficulties that confront every pioneer. The railway men thought he was a hare-brained fool. His own father refused to lend him any money for such child's-play as an air-brake.

Westinghouse tramped from one railway office to another, and was treated as a mild lunatic by most railway managers. "Stopping a train by wind! What next!"

At last he found a railway man who had courage and sense — W. W. Card, of the Panhandle Railway.

Mr. Card agreed to allow Westinghouse to make a trial, on condition that he paid all his own expenses.

By this time Westinghouse had no money at all, but he agreed. Then he ran around among his friends and borrowed every penny he could get. A young man named Ralph Baggaley gave him the most help at this time.

A trial run was made. The driver was a keen young man named Daniel Tate; and just before the start, Westinghouse tipped Tate a $50 note.

"Give the brake a fair chance, Dan," he said. This was all the money that Westinghouse had, and it was borrowed.

Then came a bit of pure luck. The trial train was running at thirty miles an hour when a teamster drove across the track a short distance in front. The driver lashed the horses, but they reared backwards and flung him between the rails.

Tate turned on the air-brake. The train stopped — four feet from the prostrate driver. Such was the sensational *début* of the air-brake. After that, there were plenty of orders and plenty of $50 notes.

Three years later, Westinghouse visited England and had a second battle with railway managers. His best friend was *Engineering*, which took his side from the first. And his first order came from the Metropolitan District Railway of London.

By 1881 the air-brake had become the standard brake. Westinghouse had a large factory at Pittsburg. At thirty-five he had become rich and famous.

He lived thirty-three years longer and every year was packed with new ideas and inventions. He plunged into electrical work and gas engines. He grew new factories as a farmer grows corn.

As his men said, "No one can ever guess where the Old Man will break out next."

He was not spoiled by his success. He was strong-willed and dominating, as every strong man must be; but HE NEVER LOST TOUCH WITH HIS WORKERS.

His workers were more loyal to him than his bankers and he lost the financial control of his business.

Once his workers offered to take half-pay, because they knew he was in need of money. At another time his men raised $600,000 to help him carry on at a time when he was pinched.

Earnest, tense, honest, fair, aggressive, optimistic, energetic, courageous — such was George Westinghouse. He was proud of his workmen. He trained them and worked beside them. He loved work and working people. And when he died in 1914, his pall-bearers were eight old mechanics, who had been his fellow-workers for more than forty years.

CPSIA information can be obtained
at www.ICGtesting.com
Printed in the USA
LVHW022132220123
737717LV00014B/1169